Creative Christmas Programs

Creative Christmas Programs

For Sunday Schools and Church Groups

Jerry Koetje

BAKER BOOK HOUSE
Grand Rapids, Michigan 49516

Copyright 1991 by
Baker Book House Company

ISBN: 0-8010-5297-1

Scripture passages are from the New International Version
© 1978 by New York Bible Society.
Printed in the United States of America

Without securing further permission, local churches are allowed to duplicate one copy of a specific program for the use of each participant.

This book is dedicated
to my wonderful wife,
Kris,
who has supported and encouraged me
to share these ideas with you.

Contents

Preface   9
Introduction   11
Notes for Program Directors   13
Christmas Program Checklist   15
Organizational Chart   17

1. Jesus Our King   19
2. Hear the Bells   37
3. The Mission   55
4. Prince of Peace   73
5. The Light of Jesus   97
6. The Lamb   115
7. Happy Birthday, Jesus   133
8. Of Men and Angels   157

Preface

Have you ever felt frustrated with the quality of Christmas programs? Have you ever wondered if children could relate to more than a mere baby in the manger? Because of a dearth of participation, creativity, or music ability some children's Christmas programs are shallow and lack excitement and enthusiasm.

Many church workers have the annual, seemingly overwhelming task of pulling Christmas material together to form a program for children to present to adults in a worship service. This book has been compiled after twelve years of research and experience in local churches. I know the children will enjoy performing these programs and many people will leave with the challenge to begin or continue a committed walk with God as Savior and Lord.

Introduction

My aunt, Jean Koetje, has inspired and encouraged me to write materials for children. These programs are intended to bring praise and glory to God through children. They present the whole gospel of Christ to the congregation on a level children can understand while also communicating effectively to adults. When children understand the message and become excited about it, then adults, especially those who don't regularly attend church, will be able to hear and respond to the good news of the Christmas events.

The goal of these programs is to present God at work in the world of yesterday, today, and tomorrow. Too often we isolate Jesus merely as a baby in a manger and the message of God at work in the world seems to begin and end with Jesus as a baby. These programs have a fresh perspective as the totality of our Lord's ministry is dramatized. Each program begins in the Old Testament and anticipates the coming Messiah. Next Jesus' birth, life, death, and resurrection are presented. The program closes by showing how Jesus is alive and at work in our world today.

Notes for Program Directors

Begin early in the fall to plan and delegate the work involved. Save the props from year to year because many can be used again. Included in this book is a checklist of items to monitor each week. There is also a chart showing how to organize a staff to help direct the program. If your church is small, combine responsibilities. If your church is larger, add or divide the responsibilities. It is my hope and prayer God will use your church program as an instrument to bring his gospel to a world desperately looking for answers.

Parts

Each program has a number of assigned parts. Every year the number of children involved varies. As director you need to decide how many parts are needed for the ages involved. Here are a few suggestions. If your goal is to have an individual part for each child in church, then parts may be added or deleted by giving or taking away lines from the narrator(s). Another suggestion is to have children say lines as a group of choral readers. Children are the key to the success of the program. Be sure as many individuals as possible have lines to say. Parents will come out to hear their children speak, act, or sing. Older children can serve as narrators and movers of props and scenery.

Delegation

When a program director tries to run the program alone, that leads to much work and frustration. I have found teachers are more than willing to help when asked. However, the director needs to give clear directions regarding the tasks assigned. Teachers can lead in music, props, and the sound/lights areas. Follow up to make sure the task is carried out. Delegating responsibilities to others allows people to feel needed.

Program Rehearsals

Help the children and leaders to focus on the flow of the program, not on part memorization. Sometimes too much time is taken helping a child learn a part when others are waiting for their turn to say parts. It is more helpful at practices to have the children *and* leaders know the order of spoken parts, where children sit, when they speak, and when they sing.

Ask teachers and leaders to be involved with the children by helping with parts and singing so the children know when to speak and sing. The teachers and leaders can be lining up children in their seats and working on part memorization, while the director focuses on maintaining the flow of the program.

Practice in small groups early in December. As the program date gets closer, practice as an entire group. Three practice days should be enough. The first two are with smaller groups and last about one hour. The last practice is with the entire group. Allow 1 1/2 to 2 hours for the large group to go through the entire program twice.

It works best to have children not come too early on the day of the program to run through a major rehearsal. Small children have short attention spans and too much energy to sit through the practice *and* the program. It is better if the children do not rehearse and perform back to back. Everyone should arrive at least forty-five minutes to an hour ahead of the starting time to organize and go over last-minute details.

Christmas Program Checklist

10 weeks ahead
_____ Appoint a director
_____ Choose a program
_____ Pray each week for the children and leaders involved

9 weeks ahead (the director lines up the key staff personnel)
_____ Music Director
_____ Three-year-old through first grade leader
_____ Second- through fifth-grade leader
_____ Sixth- through eighth-grade leader
_____ Props leader
_____ Lights and sound leader

8 weeks ahead
_____ Set program practice dates
_____ Meet with the staff
_____ Begin working on the props and costumes
_____ Assign parts to children
_____ Distribute copies of the program to all the teachers, leaders, and persons involved in the program with children's names written in by the assigned parts
_____ Arrange for music with the music leader

6 weeks ahead
_____ Select soloist or other special music persons and tapes

_____ Continue working on props and costumes
_____ Remind leaders of the program practice dates

4 weeks ahead
_____ Have teachers hand out parts to children
_____ Arrange for a person to videotape the program
_____ Meet with the staff to discuss progress and needs

3 weeks ahead
_____ Begin program practices
_____ Complete the props and costumes

2 weeks ahead
_____ Continue program practices
_____ Have the children try on the costumes to be sure sizes are correct
_____ Use props in practices

1 week ahead
_____ Have dress rehearsals with the children and leaders including costumes, sound, lights, and props
_____ When practicing is finished, collect all props and costumes and hold them until the day of the program

1 week after the program
_____ Send thank-you notes to key personnel involved in the program

Organizational Chart

- **Program Director**
  - **Music leader**
    - Pianist(s)
    - Organist
    - Special Music
    - Instrumentalists
  - **Three-year-olds through first grade leader**
    - Teachers
    - Helpers
  - **Second through fifth grade leader**
    - Teachers
    - Helpers
  - **Sixth through eighth grade leader**
    - Teachers
    - Helpers
  - **Sound and Lights**
    - V.C.R. Taping
  - **Props**
    - Scenery
    - Costumes

1

Jesus Our King

Notes to the Director

Find a "Dad" speaker who can speak clearly and slowly enough to be understood.

The "Son" and "Dad" need not be related.

The father and son could narrate either from the balcony or the side of the stage.

They must be able to see the program in progress.

Speaking parts can be added or deleted according to class size.

Songs may be added or deleted according to your church tradition. Please do so according to the content and flow of the action in the program.

Closing: There are two options given. Follow the traditions of your church. It is important that people feel personally challenged to receive Christ as Savior, Lord, and King.

List of Characters

Three- and Four-Year-Olds

Child one
Child two
Child three

Child four
Child five

Five-Year-Olds

Speaker one
Speaker two
Speaker three
Speaker four
Speaker five
Speaker six
Speaker seven
Speaker eight
Speaker nine
Speaker ten
Speaker eleven
Speaker twelve
Speaker thirteen

First–Third Graders

Choral Readers 1
Choral Readers 2
Wise Men

Fourth Graders

Speaker one: Luke 19:38
Speaker two: Luke 23:3
Speaker three: Luke 23:35
Speaker four: Luke 23:36–37
Speaker five: Luke 23:38
Speaker six: Luke 23:39
Speaker seven: Luke 23:40–41
Speaker eight: Luke 23:42–43

Fifth Graders

Speaker one: 1 Corinthians 1:18
Speaker two: 1 Corinthians 1:19

Speaker three: 1 Corinthians 1:20
Speaker four: 1 Corinthians 1:21
Speaker five: 1 Corinthians 1:22–23
Speaker six: 1 Corinthians 1:24
Speaker seven: 1 Corinthians 1:25

Additional Characters

Adult Dad, Son, Isaiah, Herod, Angel 1, Mary, Elizabeth, Zechariah, Angel 2, Chief Priest 1, Chief Priest 2, Adult Speaker—Revelation 19:11–16, Teachers (5)—nonspeaking role

Props

Introduction to Program

Letters made from cardboard with the program theme

JESUS OUR KING

The Program

Two angel costumes are necessary.

Costumes from bathrobes or sheets need to be made for the following:

1. Mary
2. Elizabeth
3. Zechariah
4. Joseph
5. Wise Men (purple, red, or multi-colored robes)
6. Herod (purple and white robe)
7. Chief Priest (bright, colored robe)
8. Teachers

Dad and son dress in choir robes, if available; otherwise, ordinary apparel usually worn to church

Choral readers dress in choir robes, if available; otherwise, white shirts/blouses with dark skirts/pants

...kers one to eight of the fourth grade and speakers ...even of the fifth grade dress in clothing usually worn to church.

A background scene resembling a room in a house is necessary for the scenes involving Mary, Zechariah, and Elizabeth. The same scene could be used for Joseph and the angel and later for the Wise Men, Herod, Chief Priest, and teachers. The room should contain a chair, a couch, and a simple coffee table. A pulpit chair could be used for King Herod's throne.

Songs

Away in a Manger
The Welcome Song
Silent Night! Holy Night!
What Child Is This?
The First Noel
Hark! the Herald Angels Sing
Joy to the World
Angels, From the Realms of Glory
He's Alive
He Lives!
Now I Belong to Jesus
Hallelujah Chorus

Jesus Our King

Processional: Boys and girls march in and are seated while singing "Boys and Girls for Jesus."

Program Welcome
Three- and four-year-olds
Song: "Away in a Manger"

Welcome to Parents:

Child 1:	Jesus is my friend.
Child 2:	Jesus is my Savior.
Child 3:	Jesus is my King.
Child 4:	Do you know my Jesus?
Child 5:	Welcome to our program!
Song:	"There's a Welcome Here" or "The Welcome Song"

Introduction to the Program: Five-year-olds

Speaker 1: You may think I came up here to tell you about our church or city, but I really came to tell you that we are the welcome committee.

Speakers two through thirteen hold cards with the letters
JESUS OUR KING

Speaker 2—*J*: J is for Jesus who came from above to give us peace, and hope, and love.
Speaker 3—*E*: E is for earth, the place of Jesus' birth.
Speaker 4—*S*: S is for star, that guided wise men from afar.
Speaker 5—*U*: U is for us; Emmanuel means "God with us."
Speaker 6—*S*: S is for son: God's son Jesus, his only one.

Speaker 7—*O*: O is for open. We open our hearts to receive God's love.
Speaker 8—*U*: U is for using our voices for singing.
Speaker 9—*R*: R is for ringing the bells to show, Jesus was born so long ago.

Speaker 10—*K*:	**K** is for keeping, the Bible truths we will be singing.
Speaker 11—*I*:	**I** is for inn, a place where Mary and Joseph found no room for them.
Speaker 12—*N*:	**N** is for night, the special night when the stars shone so bright.
Speaker 13—*G*:	**G** is for glory, when God sent his angels to tell others the magnificent story.

The Program

Son:	Dad, why do we celebrate Christmas? My friend asked me this question and I don't know how to answer him.
Dad:	One reason is because the son of God, Jesus, was born then. Because of this, nearly everyone shares in the special atmosphere of Christmas. Families are reunited. The air seems filled with happiness when we give and receive gifts. Even our stores play Christmas music. Many churches have candlelight services and Christmas programs just like this to celebrate the birth of this baby in a manger.
Song:	"Silent Night! Holy Night!" sung by the three-year-olds through the fifth graders.
Son:	But, Dad, why was Jesus born?
Dad:	(Son's name), let me explain. Around 2000 years ago in a little city far away in the land of Israel, there lived a young woman named Mary.

Mary enters and goes to platform.

She was soon to be married to a carpenter named Joseph, a descendant of King David. One day Mary was sitting alone in her home.

Mary sits down.

Suddenly an angel came and spoke with her.

Angel 1: "Greetings, you who are highly favored! The Lord is with you" (Luke 1:28).

Mary: Screams and then says, "You frighten me; go away, this is my house!"

Angel 1: "Do not be afraid, Mary, you have found favor with God. You will be with child and give birth to a son, and you are to give him the name Jesus. He will be great and will be called the Son of the Most High. The Lord God will give him the throne of his father David, and he will reign over the house of Jacob forever; his kingdom will never end" (Luke 1:30–33).

Mary: "How will this be, since I am a virgin?" (Luke 1:34).

Angel 1: "The Holy Spirit will come upon you, and the power of the Most High will overshadow you. So the holy one to be born will be called the Son of God. Even Elizabeth your relative is going to have a child in her old age, and she who was said to be barren is in her sixth month. For nothing is impossible with God" (Luke 1:35–37).

Mary: "I am the Lord's servant. May it be to me as you have said" (Luke 1:38).

Mary stands and leaves the platform.

Son:	Dad, what did Mary do after the angel left?
Dad:	Well, she was very excited. (Son's name), what did you do when the coach told you you made the basketball team last week?
Son:	I went and told my best friend Tom.
Dad:	Mary did something like that too. She packed up and went to visit her relative Elizabeth. Both of them were going to have babies.

*Elizabeth enters and sits down.
Mary runs in with bags packed with clothes.*

Mary:	Elizabeth, Elizabeth, guess what!
Elizabeth:	Hi, Mary. It's good to see you!
Mary:	An angel came and told me you were going to have a baby. I wanted to come and say congratulations to you and your husband Zechariah. Is he here?

Zechariah enters.

Mary:	Congratulations, Zechariah!
Zechariah:	Why, thank you, Mary.
Mary:	Do you know what else the angel said?
Zech. and Eliza.:	No, please tell us!
Mary:	I'm going to have a baby, too!
Zech. and Eliza.:	That's wonderful! Congratulations! We're so happy for you.
Dad:	The Bible then says that when Elizabeth's baby, who was John the Baptist, heard about Mary's baby, it leaped for joy inside her. Then Elizabeth said to Mary:

Elizabeth: "Blessed are you among women, and blessed is the child you will bear! But why am I so favored, that the mother of my Lord should come to me? As soon as the sound of your greeting reached my ears, the baby in my womb leaped for joy. Blessed is she who has believed that what the Lord has said to her will be accomplished!" (Luke 1:42b–45).

Dad: To celebrate the birth of Jesus, please stand and sing "What Child Is This?"

Congregational Hymn: "What Child Is This?" (the congregation stands.)

While the congregation is singing, the children prepare to sing.

Children sing: "The First Noel" and "Hark! the Herald Angels Sing"

Choral readers stand in groups of four or five and speak together.

Choral readers 1: This is how the birth of Jesus Christ came about: His mother Mary was pledged to be married to Joseph, but before they came together, she was found to be with child through the Holy Spirit (Matt. 1:18).

Choral readers 2: Because Joseph her husband was a righteous man and did not want to expose her to public disgrace, he had in mind to divorce her quietly. But after he considered this, an angel of the Lord appeared to him in a dream and said: (Matt. 1:19–20a)

Joseph comes in and sits down. The angel of God comes in and stands by Joseph with arms raised.

Angel 2: "Joseph son of David, do not be afraid to take Mary home as your wife, because what is conceived in her is from the Holy Spirit. She will give birth to a son, and you are to give him the name Jesus, because he will save his people from their sins" (Matt. 1:20a–21).

The angel leaves and Joseph lies down.

Choral readers 1: All this took place to fulfill what the Lord had said through the prophet Isaiah (Matt. 1:22).

Isaiah: The virgin will be with child and will give birth to a son, and they will call him Immanuel, which means, "God With Us" (Matt. 1:23).

Joseph gets up. Mary comes on stage. The two join hands and walk out to the back of church.

Choral readers 2: When Joseph woke up, he did what the angel of the Lord commanded him and took Mary home as his wife (Matt. 1:24).

Choral readers 1: But he had no union with her until she gave birth to a son. And he gave him the name Jesus (Matt. 1:25).

Songs by Sunday school children: "Joy to the World" and "Angels From the Realms of Glory"

Son: Dad, Jesus is a king, isn't he? Some of my friends believe Jesus lived many years ago and was an important person then but is no longer important today.

Dad: Here are a few boys and girls whom I have asked to tell us that Jesus is still a very important person today. He is not only the king of this world but can also be the king of our lives. In the Book of Matthew we find the wise men from the east following the star to Israel. They weren't sure which city Jesus was in, so they stopped at Jerusalem to ask King Herod. Matthew tells us these words:

King Herod enters and sits on a throne, then four to six wise men enter and speak to Herod.

Wise Men: "Where is the one who has been born king of the Jews? We saw his star in the east and have come to worship him" (Matt. 2:1–2).

Herod: I don't know, but stay here; I'll go find out from my chief priests and teachers.

Herod speaks with the teachers and chief priests.

Herod: Come and tell these wise men from the East: where is the king of the Jews to be born?

Chief priests and teachers come back with Herod and tell the wise men where Jesus was born.

Herod: We have the answer to your question. My chief priests will tell you.

Chief Priest 1:	In Bethlehem in Judea. For this is what the prophet has written: (Matt. 2:5)
Chief Priest 2:	But you, Bethlehem, in the land of Judah, are by no means least among the rulers of Judah; for out of you will come a ruler who will be the shepherd of my people Israel (Matt. 2:6).
Dad:	After the wise men heard the king, they went on their way, and the star they had seen in the east went ahead of them until it stopped over the place where the child was. When they saw the star, they were overjoyed. On coming to the house, they saw the child with his mother Mary, and they bowed down and worshiped him with their gifts of gold, and of incense and of myrrh (Matt. 2:9–12). Jesus grew strong and wise. He healed the sick and taught the people many truths about God and man. The Christ Jesus, Immanuel, laid out a beautiful example of what true kingship is all about. Later in his life, one week before he was to be crucified on the cross, Jesus entered Jerusalem on a donkey. The people greeted Jesus by saying:
Speaker 1:	"Blessed is the king who comes in the name of the Lord! Peace in heaven and glory in the highest!" (Luke 19:38).
Dad:	Just hours before Jesus was to be crucified he stood before Pilate, the Roman governor of Israel. Pilate asked Jesus a very important question. Listen to (name of speaker two).

Speaker 2: So Pilate asked Jesus, "Are you the king of the Jews?" "Yes, it is as you say," Jesus replied (Luke 23:3).

Dad: When the religious leaders of Jesus' day insisted on killing Jesus, Pilate quit arguing with them and allowed Jesus to be crucified. On the cross on which Jesus died, a sign was posted saying: "This is the king of the Jews" (Matt. 23:38). Listen to my friends tell the story.

Speaker 3: The people stood watching, and the rulers even sneered at him. They said, "He saved others; let him save himself if he is the Christ of God, the Chosen One" (Luke 23:35).

Speaker 4: The soldiers also came up and mocked him. They offered him wine vinegar and said, "If you are the king of the Jews, save yourself" (Luke 23:36–37).

Speaker 5: There was a notice written above him, which read: THIS IS THE KING OF THE JEWS (Luke 23:38).

Speaker 6: One of the criminals who hung there hurled insults at him: "Aren't you the Christ? Save yourself and us!" (Luke 23:39).

Speaker 7: But the other criminal rebuked him: "Don't you fear God," he said, "Since you are under the same sentence? We are punished justly, for we are getting what our deeds deserve. But this man has done nothing wrong" (Luke 23:40–41).

Speaker 8: Then he said, "Jesus, remember me when you come into your kingdom."

	Jesus answered him, "I tell you the truth, today you will be with me in paradise" (Luke 23:42–43).
Dad:	Jesus didn't stay in the grave. After three days he arose from the grave and carries on the work of his Father in heaven. Don Francisco sang a beautiful song entitled "He's Alive." Listen to the words.
Song:	"He's Alive"—Can be played from the tape of Don Francisco or sung by a soloist.
Son:	Dad, that song is exciting. It makes me want to sing. Can we sing a song?
Dad:	Okay. Please open your hymn books to number ___, and stand together, singing "He Lives."
Congregation Sings:	"He Lives"
Dad:	We have told a powerful story about Jesus Christ, a baby who became a savior and king. His kingdom is the church of believers. So you see, son, God doesn't always react in ways that we think he should. God used a cross and death to offer us peace and life. Christ is the wisdom and power of God.
Speaker 1:	For the message of the cross is foolishness to those who are perishing, but to us who are being saved it is the power of God (1 Cor. 1:18).
Speaker 2:	For it is written: I will destroy the wisdom of the wise; the intelligent I will frustrate (1 Cor. 1:19).

Speaker 3: Where is the wise man? Where is the scholar? Where is the philosopher of this age? (1 Cor. 1:20).

Speaker 4: For since in the wisdom of God the world through its wisdom did not know him, God was pleased through the foolishness of what was preached to save those who believe (1 Cor. 1:21).

Speaker 5: Jews demand miraculous signs and Greeks look for wisdom, but we preach Christ crucified: a stumbling block to Jews and foolishness to Gentiles (1 Cor. 1:22–23).

Speaker 6: But to those whom God has called, both Jews and Greeks, Christ is the power of God and the wisdom of God (1 Cor. 1:24).

Speaker 7: For the foolishness of God is wiser than man's wisdom, and the weakness of God is stronger than man's strength (1 Cor. 1:25).

Closing

Dad: We began tonight's program by asking two questions: "Why do we celebrate Christmas?" and "Why was Jesus born?" We celebrate Christmas to rejoice in the birth of a king. The King of all kings! The Lord of all lords! It is our hope and prayer each person here tonight knows this King of kings and Lord of lords personally. If not, please see me or the pastor before you leave tonight. Someday Christ Jesus will return and make all wrongs right again. We leave you tonight with these words from Revelation 19:11–16.

Adult Speaker:	I saw heaven standing open and there before me was a white horse, whose rider is called Faithful and True. With justice he judges and makes war. His eyes are like blazing fire, and on his head are many crowns. He has a name written on him that no one knows but he himself. He is dressed in a robe dipped in blood, and his name is the Word of God. The armies of heaven were following him, riding on white horses and dressed in fine linen, white and clean. Out of his mouth comes a sharp sword with which to strike down the nations. He will rule them with an iron scepter. He treads the winepress of the fury of the wrath of God Almighty. On his robe and on his thigh he has this name written: KING OF KINGS AND LORD OF LORDS (Rev. 19:11–16).
Dad:	Please remain seated as we receive the offering for the work of Christ's church and sing our closing song "Now I Belong to Jesus."
Congregation Sings:	"Now I Belong to Jesus"
Benediction	
Postlude:	Play the song from the "Messiah" titled "Hallelujah Chorus" or have the senior choir sing this.
	Optional Closing
Dad:	We began tonight's program by asking two questions: "Why do we celebrate Christmas?" and "Why was Jesus born?"

We celebrate Christmas to rejoice in the birth of a king. The King of all kings! The Lord of all lords! It is our hope and prayer each person here tonight knows this King of kings and Lord of lords personally. If you don't know Christ the King or have lived apart from him for a time, we are going to ask you to make a decision to follow him today. When you hear the song titled " (choose a song which fits)" please come to the front of the church. Others will be with you to help commit your life to Christ. If God is pulling on your heart tonight, don't wait for another opportunity. We don't know what the future holds. Come now. God is calling you today in a way you may never hear again.

While the song is played have persons present in the front of church who are capable of leading someone to Christ and will pray with those who come forward.

Song: (Play the song here)

Dad: Someday Christ Jesus will return and make all wrongs right again. We leave you tonight with these words from Revelation 19:11–16.

Adult Speaker: I saw heaven standing open and there before me was a white horse, whose rider is called Faithful and True. With justice he judges and makes war. His eyes are like blazing fire, and on his head are many crowns. He has a name written on him that no one knows but he himself. He is dressed in a robe dipped in blood, and his name is the Word of God. The armies of heaven were following him, riding on white horses and dressed in fine linen, white and clean. Out of his mouth comes a sharp sword with which to strike down the nations. He will rule them with an iron scepter. He treads the winepress of the fury of the wrath of God Almighty. On his robe and on his thigh he has this name written: KING OF KINGS AND LORD OF LORDS (Rev. 19:11–16).

Dad: Please remain seated as we receive the offering for the work of Christ's church and sing our closing song "Now I Belong to Jesus."

Congregation
Sings: "Now I Belong to Jesus"

Benediction

Postlude: Play the song from the "Messiah" titled "Hallelujah Chorus" or have the senior choir sing this.

2

Hear the Bells

Notes to the Director

Hear the Bells is divided into the following sections:

Opening

Program welcome
Program introduction
Program theme

The Program

Old Testament family skit
"Jesus Is Coming"
New Testament story skit
"Christ Is Born"
Modern day family skit
"Go and Tell"

This allows the director the option of running the rehearsals in shifts. However, I would recommend at least one practice with everyone present.

The closing highlights area ministries. For each ministry a two- or three-sentence summary is given.

List of Characters

Opening

Child 1
Child 2
Four-year-old class
Speakers 1–12

The Program

Old Testament
Narrator
Old Testament Mom
Old Testament Dad
Child 1
Child 2
Child 3

New Testament
Joseph
Innkeeper
Mary
Angel
Shepherd 1
Shepherd 2
Shepherd 3
Shepherd 4
Narrator 2
First Prophecy
First Fulfillment
Second Prophecy
Second Fulfillment
Third Prophecy
Third Fulfillment
Fourth Prophecy

Fourth Fulfillment
Fifth Prophecy
Fifth Fulfillment
Sixth Prophecy
Sixth Fulfillment

Modern Day
Child 1
Child 2
Grandpa
Grandma
Dad
Mom
Area ministry examples:
> Loaves and Fishes' Speaker
> Youth for Christ Speaker
> Gideons' Speaker
> Salvation Army Speaker

Props
Program Introduction
Individual cardboard letters needed that spell out the words HEAR THE BELLS.

Old Testament
Mom, dad, and children should dress in Old Testament costumes (robes from sheets, blankets, bathrobes.) Colors need not match. The Jewish people often wore a wide range of contrasting colors.

The stage should be set simply with limited use of chairs and background. The focus should be on the characters and their message.

The Old Testament passages are to be read from scrolls. Use two 1" dowels, approximately 12" long. Glue the paper to the dowels. The paper should be about 8 1/2" x 14" minimum. The Scripture can be written or typed on the paper and unrolled when reading. Scrolls can be stored with a rubber band to hold sticks and paper together.

New Testament

Inn—needs a rough cut door frame.
Stable—needs a setting with a backdrop looking like cave or old wooden barn.
Manger with hay.
Shepherd staffs.
Sheep and/or other barnyard animals such as cows, goats, or donkeys made of cardboard.
Mary, mother of Jesus, should be dressed simply, in white.
Joseph and the shepherds and innkeeper should be dressed in multi-colored robes made from sheets, bedspreads, or bathrobes. Shepherds should carry staffs.
Angel costumes should be white (a halo is also needed.)

Modern Day

Modern day house background needed. Include chairs, couch, floor lamps, Christmas tree, and presents.
Signs for local ministries such as: Loaves and Fishes, Youth for Christ, etc.

Songs

Happy All the Time
Away in a Manger
O Come, All Ye Faithful
Jesus Loves Me
The B–I–B–L–E
Bells Are Ringing—Christ Will Come!

Silent Night! Holy Night!
Hark! the Herald Angels Sing
Bells Are Ringing—Christ Is Born!
Oh, How He Loves You and Me
I Will Sing the Wondrous Story
Oh, How I Love Jesus
Go Tell It On the Mountain

—Hear the Bells—

Opening
Program Welcome

Three-year-olds

Child 1: "I may be small, I'm not too tall; but my voice can shout what Jesus is all about."

Songs: "Happy All the Time"
"Away In a Manger"

Child 2: "I am only three, but I can say, 'Merry Christmas, Jesus, I love you.'"

Introduction
Four-year-olds

All children say together: "Christmas is a special day, we come to church to say: Jesus is our King; that is why we sing!"

Songs: "O Come, All Ye Faithful"
"Jesus Loves Me"

Program Theme

H is for HOPE: The hope we share in a risen King.
E is for EARTH: The place God chose to save you and me.
A is for ANGEL: The angel came to tell the good news of Jesus' birth.
R is for RINGING: Ringing the bells to tell and to show the birth of Jesus 2000 years ago.

T is for TREE: The tree Jesus died on for you and for me.
H is for HOPE: A hope for the lost to see Jesus, who died on the cross.
E is for EAR: To hear the message God sent us in his Son.

B is for BABY: Jesus came as a baby to save us from sin.
E is for EMMANUEL: This name for Jesus means "God with us."
L is for LISTENING to the stories we bring.
L is for LEARNING about Jesus our King.
S is for SINGING special songs for Jesus our Lord.

Songs: "The B–I–B–L–E"
"Bells are Ringing—Christ Will Come"

—Old Testament Family—

"Jesus Is Coming"

Narrator: The Old Testament Jews took seriously the command in Deuteronomy to tell their children of what the prophets foretold of the coming of the Messiah, a king who would rule forever. All of Israel waited for the one who was later

	to be called Jesus. Listen to this Old Testament Jewish family as they share with their children the promises of the coming Messiah.
Mom:	Time for bed, children.
Child 1:	How long do we have to wait for the Messiah to come, Mom?
Mom:	We don't know; the prophets haven't told us.
Child 2:	Tell us again what the prophets have said the Messiah will be like.
All Children:	Yes, please tell us.

Father walks in.

Dad: Okay, but then off to bed with you. Mother, please bring the scrolls.

Mother goes and gets the scrolls.

Dad: Thank you. Long ago your great, great grandfather, Isaiah, told us something of the coming Messiah. Listen to what he says: "For to us a child is born, to us a son is given, and the government will be on his shoulders. And he will be called Wonderful Counselor, Mighty God, Everlasting Father, Prince of Peace. Of the increase of his government and peace there will be no end. He will reign on David's throne and over his kingdom, establishing and upholding it with justice and righteousness from that time on and forever. The zeal of the LORD Almighty will accomplish this" (Isa. 9:6–7). Isaiah also tells us he will be born of a virgin

	and his name will be Immanuel which means, 'God with us.' This Messiah will be born in Bethlehem. We know this because of what the prophet Micah once said.
Child 1:	"But you, Bethlehem Ephrathah, though you are small among the clans of Judah, out of you will come for me one who will be ruler over Israel, whose origins are from of old, from ancient times" (Micah 5:2).
Child 3:	What kind of king will this Messiah be, Dad?
Dad:	Again we are told something great about this Messiah by Isaiah. Let me find it here. Mom, will you read this for us?
Mom:	"Who has believed our message and to whom has the arm of the Lord been revealed? He grew up before him like a tender shoot, and like a root out of dry ground. He had no beauty or majesty to attract us to him, nothing in his appearance that we should desire him. He was despised and rejected by men, a man of sorrows, and familiar with suffering. Like one from whom men hide their faces he was despised, and we esteemed him not. Surely he took up our infirmities and carried our sorrows, yet we considered him stricken by God, smitten by him, and afflicted. But he was pierced for our transgressions, he was crushed for our iniquities; the punishment that brought us peace was upon him, and by his wounds we are healed. We all, like sheep, have gone astray, each of us has

turned to his own way; and the LORD has laid on him the iniquity of us all. He was oppressed and afflicted, yet he did not open his mouth; he was led like a lamb to the slaughter, and as a sheep before her shearers is silent, so he did not open his mouth. By oppression and judgment, he was taken away. And who can speak of his descendants? For he was cut off from the land of the living; for the transgression of my people he was stricken. He was assigned a grave with the wicked, and with the rich in his death, though he had done no violence, nor was any deceit in his mouth. Yet it was the LORD'S will to crush him and cause him to suffer, and though the LORD makes his life a guilt offering, he will see his offspring and prolong his days, and the will of the LORD will prosper in his hand. After the suffering of his soul, he will see the light of life and be satisfied; by his knowledge my righteous servant will justify many, and he will bear their iniquities. Therefore I will give him a portion among the great, and he will divide the spoils with the strong, because he poured out his life unto death, and was numbered with the transgressors. For he bore the sin of many, and made intercession for the transgressors" (Isa. 53).

Dad: So, you see, children, we Jews have a hard time accepting that this Messiah will come as a king. However, his kingdom is different from other kings'. This king will suffer and even die for the sins you and I have made. Children, hear and believe. This Messiah will come soon. Now, off to bed with you.

Family leaves the scene.

—New Testament Story—
"Christ Is Born"

Songs: "Silent Night! Holy Night!"
"Hark! the Herald Angels Sing"
"Bells Are Ringing—Christ Is Born"

Narrator: Let's pick up the story as Mary and Joseph enter the city of Bethlehem looking for a room to stay in.

Mary and Joseph come in. They go to the inn and Joseph knocks on door.

Joseph: Do you have a room for my wife and me?

Innkeeper: No, the town is packed full. Even my floor space is all taken.

Joseph: We don't need much room. My wife is going to have a baby soon.

Innkeeper: Sorry, I wish I could help, but there just isn't anything.

Mary: Wait, how about another building? It doesn't have to be an inn.

Innkeeper: Well, let me see, there is this stable down the road.

Mary: That will be fine. Come, Joseph, let's go there.

Turn light off Mary and Joseph as they reach the stable, and aim the light on shepherds.

Narrator: And there were shepherds living out in the fields nearby, keeping watch over their flocks at night. An angel of the Lord appeared to them, and the glory of the Lord shone around them, and they were terrified. But the angel said to them, "Do not be afraid. I bring you good news of great joy that will be for all the people. Today in the town of David a Savior has been born to you; he is Christ the Lord. This will be a sign to you: You will find a baby wrapped in cloths and lying in a manger." Suddenly a great company of the heavenly host appeared with the angel, praising God and saying,

Angel: "Glory to God in the highest, and on earth peace to men on whom his favor rests."

Narrator: When the angels had left them and gone into heaven, the shepherds said to one another:

Shepherd 1: "Let's go to Bethlehem and see this thing that has happened, which the Lord has told us about" (Luke 2:8–15).

Shepherds go to stable and worship Jesus.

Shepherd 2: So, this is the Messiah the angels told us about.

Shepherd 3: Congratulations, Mary and Joseph!

Shepherd 4: Come shepherds, let's tell everyone else about this.

Lights go out. Scene changes to those who prophesy about Jesus and the fulfillment of prophecy.

Narrator:	The shepherds' hearts were glad as they saw with their own eyes the fulfillment of many prophecies concerning Christ. Listen as the children share a few of these with us.
Narrator 2:	Jesus is to be born of a virgin.
First Prophecy:	"Therefore the Lord himself will give you a sign: The virgin will be with child and will give birth to a son, and will call him Immanuel" (Isa. 7:14).
First Fulfillment:	In the sixth month, God sent the angel Gabriel to Nazareth, a town in Galilee, to a virgin pledged to be married to a man named Joseph, a descendant of David. The virgin's name was Mary. But the angel said to her, "Do not be afraid, Mary, you have found favor with God. You will be with child and give birth to a son, and you are to give him the name Jesus" (Luke 1:26, 27, 30, 31).
Narrator 2:	Jesus is to heal the brokenhearted.
Second Prophecy:	"The Spirit of the Sovereign LORD is on me, because the LORD has anointed me to preach good news to the poor. He has sent me to bind up the brokenhearted, to proclaim freedom for the captives and release for the prisoners, to proclaim the year of the LORD'S favor and the day of vengeance of our God, to comfort all who mourn" (Isa. 61:1–2).
Second Fulfillment:	"The Spirit of the Lord is on me, because he has anointed me to preach good news to the poor. He has sent me to proclaim freedom for the prisoners and recovery of sight for the blind, to release

	the oppressed, to proclaim the year of the Lord's favor" (Luke 4:18–19).
Narrator 2:	Jesus was rejected by some.
Third Prophecy:	"He was despised and rejected by men, a man of sorrows, and familiar with suffering. Like one from whom men hide their faces he was despised, and we esteemed him not" (Isa. 53:3).
Third Fulfillment:	"He came to that which was his own, but his own did not receive him" (John 1:11). "With one voice they cried out, 'Away with this man! Release Barabbas to us!'" (Luke 23:18).
Narrator 2:	Jesus was silent to accusations.
Fourth prophecy:	"He was oppressed and afflicted, yet he did not open his mouth" (Isa. 53:7a).
Fourth Fulfillment:	"So again Pilate asked him, 'Aren't you going to answer? See how many things they are accusing you of.' But Jesus still made no reply, and Pilate was amazed" (Mark 15:4–5).
Narrator 2:	Jesus was crucified with criminals.
Fifth Prophecy:	"Therefore I will give him a portion among the great, and he will divide the spoils with the strong, because he poured out his life unto death, and was numbered with the transgressors. For he bore the sin of many, and made intercession for the transgressors" (Isa. 53:12).
Fifth Fulfillment:	"They crucified two robbers with him, one on his right and one on his left" (Mark 15:27–28).

Narrator:	Jesus was to be resurrected.
Sixth Prophecy:	"... because you will not abandon me to the grave, nor will you let your Holy One see decay" (Ps. 16:10). "But God will redeem my soul from the grave; he will surely take me to himself" (Ps. 49:15).
Sixth Fulfillment:	"Don't be alarmed," he said. "You are looking for Jesus the Nazarene, who was crucified. He has risen! He is not here. See the place where they laid him. But go, tell his disciples and Peter, 'He is going ahead of you into Galilee. There you will see him, just as he told you'" (Mark 16:6–7). This is why it says: "When he ascended on high, he led captives in his train and gave gifts to men" (Eph. 4:8).
Solo:	"Oh, How He Loves You and Me"
Narrator:	Let us continue to praise God by opening our hymn books to "I Will Sing The Wondrous Story." Please stand as we sing.
Song:	Congregation sings "I Will Sing the Wondrous Story"

—Modern Day Family—
"Go and Tell"

Scene:	Modern day family getting ready to celebrate Christmas in living room. All family members are seated in chairs or on couch.
Child 1:	Hurry, Grandpa, sit down so we can open presents!

Child 2: Come on, Grandma, it's time to open presents!

Grandpa: Now, be patient, children. First we need to talk about the fact that it is Jesus' birthday.

Mom and Grandma come walking in with presents. They put the presents under the Christmas tree and then sit down.

Child 2: (Very excited) Look at this one. I know it's mine.

Child 1: Look at this big one. It has my name on it. I wonder what's in it. Dad, can I open it?

Dad: Not quite yet. But soon. Dad (Grandpa), why do we give presents?

Grandpa: We give presents because it is Jesus' birthday. When your Grandma and I went shopping for these presents, questions were going through our minds like: "I wonder if everyone will like what we bought for them?" and "Do you think they will be able to guess what's inside?"

Grandma: God also sent a present to us many years ago. His present was in the form of a baby named Jesus. Before God gave Jesus to the world, he may have wondered how the people on earth would receive this present named Jesus.

Mom: That's right. A long time ago God sent Jesus to earth to be born. Jesus came here so we could be forgiven of our sins. When you do naughty things, when I do naughty things, we tell

Grandma:	Jesus about them, and say we are sorry, and he forgives us for all we have done.
	God gave us a Christmas present: He gave us Jesus for our friend. We give these presents today to remind us of the fact that God gave the greatest gift ever given. God loved the world so much that he gave his only Son, Jesus, and if you and I believe on him we won't die but we will live forever with Jesus in heaven.
Dad:	The presents we open today remind us of the present God gave to the world. Let's sing a song called, "Oh, How I Love Jesus."
Song:	"Oh, How I Love Jesus"
Grandpa:	That's a very good song. Just before Jesus went to heaven, he told us to share with others the Good News that he can be the Savior and Lord to anyone who believes on him. (Child 2), will you read Acts 1:8–9 for us?
Child 2:	"**But you will receive power when the Holy Spirit comes on you; and you will be my witnesses in Jerusalem, and in all Judea and Samaria, and to the ends of the earth.**" After he said this, he was taken up before their very eyes, and a cloud hid him from their sight (Acts 1:8–9).
Grandpa:	Here in [Kalamazoo] we have many men and women who are being Jesus' witnesses to all the world. Let's listen to what is said about them.

Local Area Ministries

(These are a few examples of ministries you may wish to include.)

Loaves and Fishes: This ministry is coordinated through local churches. Loaves and Fishes distributes food free of charge to those individuals in need on an emergency basis.

Youth for Christ: Youth for Christ is part of an international organization with a local office reaching the [Kalamazoo] area unchurched young people for Christ through Bible study clubs, retreats to Florida and Colorado, and the [Kalamazoo] juvenile home. Over 200 young people have prayed to make a personal commitment to Christ this past year. These youth are then funnelled into area local churches to receive training in God's word.

Gideons: The Gideons are most noted for placing Bibles in the travel resorts, hospitals, and schools. They work throughout the year obtaining Bibles and Christian literature to be distributed in places where persons may normally not hear the gospel of Christ.

Salvation Army: The Salvation Army raises money for local needy children. You may see them collecting money at the Christmas holiday season by ringing bells at local merchant doors. Some of these monies buy Christmas presents for local needy boys and girls. Last year the Salvation Army also served over 800 young women in 13 area counties through four vital programs that make up what they call "Booth Services."

Dad: We all need to continue to share the good news of Jesus with those we come in contact with each day. God's ministry didn't begin and end in the manger or on the cross. It is alive and continues today in the hearts and lives of his people. Let's end the service with a song titled "Go Tell It on the Mountain." Please remain seated as the offering is taken during the singing of this song. Sing *ONLY* the last verse of "Go Tell It on the Mountain" standing and remain standing for the benediction.

Song: Congregation sings "Go Tell it On the Mountain" while offering is taken.

Closing remarks and benediction by the pastor

Postlude

3

The Mission

Notes to the Director

The welcome songs and speaking parts are done by the three- through five-year-olds.

The program introduction is done by the kindergarten class or the four-year-olds if needed.

The prophecy part is done by the first through third graders.

The New Testament scene with Mary, Joseph, Angel One and Angel Two is done by the first through third graders.

The birth of Jesus part is done by the first through third graders. There are twenty speaking parts. Each part may be read by a child (or combine several verses as needed.) The parts of the group of shepherds, the group of angels and the single angel are all nonspeaking parts. These may be filled in as needed from various classes or age groups.

The *Our Mission* scene should be done by fourth and fifth graders.

The *Missionary Scene at Church* should be done by fifth and sixth graders.

High school age youth are used for the parts of Old Testament father and for the modern day father and mother.

Need a soloist to sing either "Redeeming Love" or "My Soul Doth Magnify the Lord." Also need a soloist to sing

"Come, Thou Long Expected Jesus" and a piano soloist to play "Blessed Redeemer."

Two narrators are needed for this program; one for the Scripture reading and one for the story narration.

The pastor could give a ten-minute talk on the innkeeper's perspective.

When you reach the *Missionary Speaker* section of the program, the children should dress according to the culture and country they are representing. Write the missionaries of your church and look up the area in which they serve to find out what type of dress the natives in the area wear.

List of Characters

Welcome
Five speaking parts

Program Introduction
Ten speaking parts

Narrators
One for the Scripture reading
One for the story narration

Old Testament Skit
Five speaking parts
Old Testament father (high school age youth)
Old Testament sons—three to five sons: a nonspeaking role

New Testament Skit
Mary
Joseph
Angel 1
Angel 2

Jesus' Birth Skit

Up to twenty speaking parts
Group of shepherds (three to five nonspeaking parts)
Angel 3: nonspeaking part
Group of angels 9 (three to five nonspeaking parts)

Our Mission

Seven speaking parts

Missionary Scene at Church

The number of speakers depends on the number of missionaries your church sponsors.

Props

Program Welcome

Speaker 5 holds a candle or flashlight.

Program Introduction

Individual cardboard letters needed that spell out "THE MISSION"

Prophecy

The children need Old Testament costumes made of sheets, bedspreads, or robes. Colors need not match. The Jewish people often wore a wide range of contrasting colors.

New Testament and Birth of Jesus

Mary, mother of Jesus, should be dressed simply, in white. Angel costumes should also be white—halos and wings are optional. Joseph should be dressed in a multicolored robe. Shepherds should be dressed in multi-colored robes—they need to carry staffs and sheep; the sheep can be made of cardboard and put on a wood floor stand. Cross—a cross needs to be made visible to the congregation with the capability to dim all church lights except for a small light on the cross.

Modern Day

Armor of God—the armor can be made or rented from a local college or high school drama department. Some magic shops also carry clothes and props which can be rented.

Sound the Battle Cry

An individual in the church plays reveille (army morning wake-up call) and the soldiers enter.

Missionaries

Missionaries may dress as one would in the country your missionary comes from.

Songs

Silent Night! Holy Night!
Away in a Manger
Jesus Loves Me
My Soul Doth Magnify the Lord
Hark! the Herald Angels Sing
O Little Town of Bethlehem
Joy to the World
The First Noel
Blessed Redeemer
He Lives
Sound the Battle Cry
Onward, Christian Soldiers
He Is Lord
Come, Thou Long-Expected Jesus

The Mission
Program Welcome

Processional:	Boys and girls from three years old through fifth grade march in singing.
Welcome:	The welcome songs and speaking parts are done by the three-through five-year-olds.

Welcome Songs: "Silent Night" (one verse)
                 "Away in a Manger" (one verse)

Speaker 1:   Jesus loves me, this I know
Speaker 2:   For the Bible tells me so
Speaker 3:   Little ones to him belong:
Speaker 4:   We are weak, but he is strong.

Song: "Jesus Loves Me" (two verses)

Speaker 5:   We want to welcome you to our program tonight, we hope it will show you about God's light.

Program Introduction

Each child holds a card on which is a letter and picture corresponding with the speaking part.

Child 1: T is for the TREE on which Jesus died for me.
Child 2: H is for HEAVEN, a place where God will take his own.
Child 3: E is for EMMANUEL, meaning God with us.

Child 4: M is for MARY, the mother of baby Jesus.
Child 5: I is for INFANT, God's son, Jesus, who came to save us.
Child 6: S is for the STAR that guided wise men from afar.
Child 7: S is for the SONGS the angels sang.
Child 8: I is for the INN, where there was no room for them.
Child 9: O is for ONE; one day Jesus will come for me.
Child 10: N is for NIGHT, with stars shining bright.

Three- to five-year-olds sit down.

Old Testament Prophecy

First through third grades

Turn lights out.

Narrator 1: In the beginning was the Word, and the Word was with God, and the Word was God. He was with God in the beginning. Through him all things were made; without him nothing was made that has been made. In him was life, and that life was the light of men. The light shines in the darkness, but the darkness has not understood it (John 1:1–5).

Lights come on slowly.

Narrator 2: Before Jesus came into the world as the perfect man-God, the Jews in the nation of Israel taught truths from the Bible in the family structure through oral tradition and memorization. Listen now as we hear a father teaching his sons about the prophecies of Isaiah regarding the coming of Jesus:

Old Testament father and group of sons stand together center stage.

Old Testament Father: Listen, my sons, and plant these truths in your hearts. The prophet Isaiah tells us:

5 Speakers (first through third graders) stand off to side of stage.

Speaker 1:	For to us a child is born, to us a son is given, and the government will be on his shoulders (Isa. 9:6a).
Speaker 2:	And he will be called Wonderful Counselor, Mighty God, Everlasting Father, Prince of Peace (Isa. 9:6b).
Speaker 3:	Of the increase of his government and peace there will be no end (Isa. 9:7a).
Speaker 4:	He will reign on David's throne and over his kingdom, establishing and upholding it with justice and righteousness from that time on and forever (Isa. 9:7b).
Speaker 5:	The zeal of the LORD Almighty will accomplish this (Isa. 9:7c).
Old Testament Father:	You see, my sons, God has a mission which is greater than any mission you and I may have. There is one to come whose reign will be better than King David's. He will bring peace to our lives. He will be strong. And he will listen to our problems and provide answers which are true.
Narrator 1:	The Jews' hope for a Messiah was passed down from father to son for many generations.

Pause and switch scenes.

New Testament Scene

Narrator 1:	In the little city of Nazareth there lived a young woman whose name was Mary. She was soon to be married to a carpenter named Joseph, who

was a descendant of David. One day Mary was sitting alone in her home when an angel of God came to her and said:

Mary comes in and sits down.

Narrator 2:	"Greetings, you who are highly favored! The Lord is with you."
Mary:	"What do you mean 'The Lord is with me?' Are you trying to scare me? Your words make me afraid."
Narrator 2:	"Do not be afraid, Mary, you have found favor with God. You will be with child and give birth to a son, and you are to give him the name Jesus. He will be great and will be called the Son of the Most High. The Lord God will give him the throne of his father David, and he will reign over the house of Jacob forever; his kingdom will never end" (Luke 1:30).
Mary:	"How will this be, since I am not married?"
Narrator 2:	"Everything will be alright. God will be the baby's father. Your baby will be called the Son of God."
Mary:	"I am the Lord's servant. May it be to me as you have said."
Narrator 1:	This was the baby promised by the Old Testament prophets. The people of God had waited many years for this event. After the angel went back to heaven, Mary was filled with joy. Mary went to find Joseph to tell him the wonderful news.

Mary runs to Joseph who is coming onto the stage.

Mary:	"Joseph, Joseph, guess what has happened?"
Joseph:	"Oh, Mary, I don't feel like playing games today."
Mary:	"I'm not playing games. I'm going to have a baby."
Joseph:	"I don't believe it. We aren't even married yet."
Mary:	"The angel of God came and told me. The angel said the baby was going to be God's Son, and he will be our King."
Joseph:	"I don't believe you. I haven't seen any angel. Now leave me."

Joseph goes and lies down.
Mary crosses stage and sits down.

Narrator 1:	It was hard for Joseph to believe Mary's words. He thought perhaps it might be better not to take Mary as his wife after all. He just couldn't understand how such a thing could happen. After Joseph had thought about this, an angel of the Lord came and spoke to him in a dream and said:
Angel 1:	"Joseph son of David, do not be afraid to take Mary home as your wife, because what is conceived in her is from the Holy Spirit" (Matt. 1:20b).
Angel 2:	"She will give birth to a son, and you are to give him the name Jesus, because he will save his people from their sins" (Matt. 1:21).

Joseph gets up and walks over to Mary.

Narrator 1:	Then Joseph was happy too. He took Mary as his wife and together they waited for this wonderful child to be born. Mary's joy overflowed into a beautiful song.
Solo:	"Redeeming Love" or "My Soul Doth Magnify the Lord" is sung by a soloist.

Set up stage for Jesus' birth.

Birth and Life of Jesus

Twenty children (see director's notes) read verses from Luke 2:1–20. This is done from the pulpit while program proceeds.

Child 1:	In those days Caesar Augustus issued a decree that a census should be taken of the entire Roman world.
Child 2:	This was the first census that took place while Quirinius was governor of Syria.
Child 3:	And everyone went to his own town to register.
Child 4:	So Joseph also went up from the town of Nazareth in Galilee to Judea, to Bethlehem the town of David, because he belonged to the house and line of David.
Child 5:	He went there to register with Mary, who was pledged to be married to him and was expecting a child.
Child 6:	While they were there, the time came for the baby to be born.
Child 7:	And she gave birth to her firstborn, a son. She wrapped him in cloths and

Meditation:	placed him in a manger, because there was no room for them in the inn.
	"The Innkeeper"—The pastor gives a ten-minute talk on the innkeeper's perspective.
Songs:	Singing to be done by all Sunday school children, standing and facing the congregation. "Hark! the Herald Angels Sing" (three verses) and "O Little Town of Bethlehem" (Children sing the first verse; the congregation joins them on verses 2–4).

Shepherds and sheep enter the stage.

Child 8:	And there were shepherds living out in the fields nearby, keeping watch over their flocks at night.
Child 9:	An angel of the Lord appeared to them, and the glory of the Lord shone around them, and they were terrified.
Child 10:	But the angel said to them, "Do not be afraid. I bring you good news of great joy that will be for all the people."
Child 11:	"Today in the town of David a Savior has been born to you; he is Christ the Lord."
Child 12:	"This will be a sign to you: You will find a baby wrapped in cloths and lying in a manger."
Child 13:	Suddenly a great company of the heavenly host appeared with the angel, praising God and saying,
Child 14:	"Glory to God in the highest, and on earth peace to men on whom his favor rests."
Child 15:	When the angels had left them and

	gone into heaven, the shepherds said to one another, "Let's go to Bethlehem and see this thing that has happened, which the Lord has told us about."
Child 16:	So they hurried off and found Mary and Joseph, and the baby, who was lying in the manger.
Songs:	Singing to be done by all Sunday school children, standing and facing the congregation. "Joy to the World" (verse 1), "The First Noel" (verse 1).
Child 17:	When they had seen him, they spread the word concerning what had been told them about this child.
Child 18:	And all who heard it were amazed at what the shepherds said to them.
Child 19:	But Mary treasured up all these things and pondered them in her heart.
Child 20:	The shepherds returned, glorifying and praising God for all the things they had heard and seen, which were just as they had been told.

Shepherds go back to sheep for a moment.
(spotlight) Clear platform after lights go out.

Narrator 1:	The children have just told us about one of the greatest births ever recorded in history: the birth of Jesus, God's Son. Through a humble birth God entered the world to accomplish a great mission. Jesus came to set all wrongs right, to offer hope and justice to a lost and misguided world. Jesus came to bring peace and love to those

	who would receive him. To reach these ideals, God had to go into battle with Satan. One of Jesus' main goals in accomplishing God's mission is told to us in the words of the apostles Luke and John.
Narrator 2:	The reason the Son of God appeared was to destroy the devil's work (1 John 3:8). "For the Son of Man came to seek and to save what was lost" (Luke 19:10).
Narrator 1:	Yes, this baby Jesus is the perfect god-man, the second person of the godhead who has volunteered to represent God fully in God's final destruction of Satan's power. The war between God and Satan had been going on since the fateful day when man, represented in Adam, the father of us all, fell into sin and became the servant of Satan. This baby is God's army. With this baby, God would ultimately destroy the evil one and bring him down from his throne. Jesus appeared to destroy Satan's claim. How? By living in this world for only thirty-three years and giving his life on Calvary's cross for my sin, for your sin. Three days later Jesus rose again, conquering sin and death forever.
Piano Solo:	"Blessed Redeemer" (Lights on cross only)
Narrator 1:	Jesus has broken Satan's power by his life, death, and resurrection. Today he lives in heaven, but his Holy Spirit is right here with us in this world helping us to fight the battle of sin. Yes, Jesus

	is alive in our world, just as much as when he walked and talked with people many years ago. Please open your hymn books to #_____ and stand together, singing "He Lives." We as Christians have much to celebrate. This song is one way of expressing our thanks to God.
Song:	"He Lives" (Congregation stands and sings)

During the singing of this song the "armor of God" kids come up from their pew and the "missionary" kids go out to a side room and come out one at a time.

Our Mission

Narrator 1:	We have just heard how Jesus came into the world with the mission of destroying the works of the devil and saving those who are lost. All who believe in Jesus are given weapons to use in the fight against Satan and his helpers. We are called to "Put on this Christian armor" in Ephesians 6.
Narrator 1:	After Jesus rose from the grave, he gave one final mission to the disciples before ascending to heaven. The children will tell us what the mission was and still is.
Child 1:	Then Jesus came to them and said, "All authority in heaven and on earth has been given to me."
Child 2:	"Therefore go and make disciples of all nations, baptizing them in the name of

	the Father and of the Son and of the Holy Spirit."
Narrator:	Then one of Jesus' disciples asked him:
Child 3:	"Lord, are you at this time going to restore the kingdom to Israel?"
Narrator:	Jesus told his listeners:
Child 4:	"It is not for you to know the times or dates the Father has set by his own authority."
Child 5:	"But you will receive power when the Holy Spirit comes on you."
Child 6:	"And you will be my witnesses in Jerusalem, and in all Judea and Samaria, and to the ends of the earth."
Narrator:	After he said this, he was taken up before their very eyes, and a cloud hid him from their sight. They were looking intently up into the sky as he was going, when suddenly two men dressed in white stood beside them.
Child 7:	"Men of Galilee," they said, "Why do you stand here looking into the sky? This same Jesus, who has been taken from you into heaven, will come back in the same way you have seen him go into heaven."
Narrator:	Our mission for God remains the same for us today. We are to begin sharing the good news of Jesus with the Samaritans in the area, namely, the neighbors in our communities. Then we need to reach out to the Jerusalems of today—the cities near us. Lastly we reach out to the world far away from us, the ends of the earth, as Acts 1:8 has told us. At our

church we sponsor missionaries who share the good news of Jesus with those who don't know God. Listen now as the children tell us about the different missionaries sponsored by our church.

Missionary Scene at Church

Have children dress according to the culture they represent.

Here are a few examples:

Missionary 1: Harry and Patricia Miersma. My name is_____. I represent Harry and Patricia Miersma from Papua New Guinea. Harry and Patricia Miersma work under the direction of Wycliffe Bible Translators, whose field organization is the Summer Institute of Linguistics. In June, 1985, they moved to Papua New Guinea, the easternmost part of the group of islands which form Indonesia, located to the north of Australia in the Coral Sea. Harry and Pat counsel individuals and families. They also lead groups, workshops and seminars on various aspects of interpersonal relationships.

Missionary 2: Thomas and Elizabeth Stewart. My name is _____. I represent Thomas and Elizabeth Stewart from Stillwater, Oklahoma. Tom and Liz Stewart have worked since 1980 as missionaries with the 1800 international students from 90 countries who attend classes at Oklahoma State University (OSU) in Stillwater. Tom compares the opportunity to minister to students from so many different countries to that of Peter on the day of Pentecost who told the good news in Jerusalem to those who had gathered there from many nations. Those who believed took the good news home with them.

Missionary 3: Arlene Schuiteman. My name is _____. I represent Arlene Schuiteman from the continent of Africa. For more than a quarter of a century, Arlene Schuiteman has served in the Sudan, Ethiopia, and Zambia. At present, she is director of the school of nursing at Macha Mission Hospital in Choma, Zambia.

Narrator: Today we still need to reach others with the mission sent from God: the mission of bringing the good news of Jesus to others we meet each day in the place we live. Whether we live in New Guinea, or Africa, or [Portage, Michigan], the mission is the same. Jesus came into the world to find and save those who are lost, those who don't know him in a personal way. You are invited to stand and join us in singing "He is Lord." The words are printed on the overhead screen.

Song: "Our God Reigns" or "He Is Lord"

For congregational singing, have the words either printed in the bulletin or on overhead screen for all people to see. All lights are out except the light to the overhead projector.

Closing

All lights out. This is sung by a soloist.

Come, Thou long-expected Jesus,
Born to set Thy people free:
From our fears and sins release us:
Let us find our rest in Thee.

Born Thy people to deliver,
Born a child, and yet a King,
Born to reign in us forever,
Now Thy gracious Kingdom bring.

By Thine own eternal Spirit,
Rule in all our hearts alone;
By Thine all-sufficient merit,
Raise us to Thy glorious throne. AMEN!

Turn lights on.

Benediction

Organ postlude

4

Prince of Peace

Notes to the Director

The narration may be done by an adult or Sunday school child who can speak slowly and clearly.

Half of the children need flowers (carnations) to hold when entering church.

A drummer should play a systematic beat for the children to march to as they enter.

Have older children play the role of Shepherd One and Shepherd Two in the *Birth of Jesus* section.

Have younger children play the Children role in the *Birth of Jesus* section.

The figure of Jesus can be portrayed from behind a curtain with proper lighting so the congregation can see the shadows of a person moving about.

Children 1 through 12 in the *Closing* need flowers around their necks and in their hands when speaking.

Flowers are given to the congregation by the Sunday school children during the closing song "Meaning of Love."

Props

Introduction

Half of the children should be dressed in army fatigues with play guns and swords, the other half should wear suits and dresses with flowers around their necks and/or in their hands.

The children with swords and guns carry signs or banners saying: "War."

The children with flowers carry signs or banners saying: "Peace."

Fall of Man into Sin

A large play snake or a picture of a snake
Fruit (apple) from the Tree of Knowledge of Good and Evil
Costumes for Adam and Eve with fig leaves drawn or clipped on them

Story of Cain and Abel

Club for Cain

Looking for Peace

Speakers 1 through 12 each need to hold a card with one letter on it which, when all put together, spells:

WE WANT PEACE!

1: **W**
2: **E**

3: **W**
4: **A**
5: **N**
6: **T**

7: **P**
8: **E**
9: **A**
10: **C**
11: **E**
12: **!**

Birth of Jesus

Costumes for the children dressed as shepherds and sheep
Manger for baby Jesus
Staff and slingshot
Stable setting
Costumes for six angels (five are nonspeaking roles)
Costumes for Mary and Joseph (nonspeaking roles)

Jesus Brings Peace

Swords for Matthew and John
Costumes for Jesus and for the children who sit with Jesus
Costume for Thomas

The Message by the Pastor

Costume for the pastor

Closing

Children 1 through 12 need a flower in their hands and a ring of flowers around their necks

List of Characters

Opening

Narrator
The children all enter from the rear of church. Half go down one aisle, the other half go down a different aisle.
A drummer

Fall of Man

Voice of the serpent
Adam
Eve
Voice of God

Story of Cain and Abel

Voice of God
Cain
Abel

Looking for Peace

Speakers 1 through 12
Child 1 through 4

Birth of Jesus

Shepherd 1
Shepherd 2
Child 1
Child 2
Children to play the roles of sheep
Angel 1
Angel Host (nonspeaking roles)
Mary (nonspeaking role)
Joseph (nonspeaking role)

Jesus Brings Peace

Matthew
John

Jesus Brings Peace (Continued)

Man dressed as Jesus
Children to sit around Jesus
Thomas

Message by the Pastor

Peter
Speaker One

Closing

Child 1 through 12

Optional: Soloist—"It Is Well With My Soul" and/or "Meaning of Love"

Songs

While Shepherds Watched Their Flocks by Night
Angels from the Realms of Glory
Hark! the Herald Angels Sing
Silent Night! Holy Night!
What Child Is This?
Jesus Is All the World to Me
I've Got Peace Like a River
It Is Well With My Soul
Meaning of Love

Opening

Two groups of children enter church from the back and proceed to the front. The first group is dressed as if going to war with helmets, swords, guns, knives, shields, army uniforms, etc. This group should represent warriors from the Old Testament day to warriors of modern times. They enter church marching and chanting: "We want war," "We want war."

The second group enters church wearing casual clothes with bands of flowers around their necks. This group should also have long-stemmed flowers in hand to give to the congregation as they enter. As they enter they chant: "We want peace," "We want peace." Both groups enter simultaneously but on opposite sides or aisles of the church. A beating drum helps the children march as they enter.

When the groups meet at the front of the church, the children stay with their group, but face the opposing group chanting "War!" "Peace!" louder each time.

Group 1:	War
Group 2:	Peace
Group 1:	*War*
Group 2:	*Peace*
Group 1:	*War!*
Group 2:	*Peace!*
Group 1:	**War**
Group 2:	**Peace**
Group 1:	**War!**
Group 2:	**Peace!**
Group 1:	***War!***
Group 2:	***Peace!***
Narrator:	We talk of peace. We speak of war. Two opposing terms. Two conflicting ideas. Yet both exist in the world. Why do we have wars? Where did all this hatred begin? To find the answer we turn to Genesis 3.

Fall of Man into Sin

Narrator:	Now the serpent was more crafty than any of wild animals the LORD God had made. He said to the woman,
Serpent:	"Did God really say, 'You must not eat from any tree in the garden'?"
Eve:	"We may eat fruit from the trees in the garden, but God did say, 'You must not eat fruit from the tree that is in the middle of the garden, and you must not touch it, or you will die.'"
Serpent:	"You will not surely die, for God knows that when you eat of it your eyes will be opened, and you will be like God, knowing good and evil."

Narrator: When the woman saw that the fruit of the tree was good for food and pleasing to the eye, and also desirable for gaining wisdom, she took some and ate it. She also gave some to her husband, who was with her, and he ate it. Then the eyes of both of them were opened, and they realized they were naked; so they sewed fig leaves together and made coverings for themselves (Gen. 3:6–7).

Pause

Narrator: Then the man and his wife heard the sound of the LORD God as he was walking in the garden in the cool of the day, and they hid from the LORD God among the trees of the garden (Gen. 3:8).

Voice of God: "[Adam], where are you?"

Adam: "I heard you in the garden, and I was afraid because I was naked; so I hid."

Voice of God: "Who told you that you were naked? Have you eaten from the tree that I commanded you not to eat from?"

Adam: "The woman you put here with me—she gave me some fruit from the tree, and I ate it."

Eve: "The serpent deceived me, and I ate."

Voice of God: So the LORD God said to the serpent, "Because you have done this, Cursed are you above all the livestock and all the wild animals! You will crawl on your belly and you will eat dust all the days of your life. And I will put enmity between

	you and the woman, and between your offspring and hers; he will crush your head, and you will strike his heel." To the woman he said, "I will greatly increase your pains in childbearing; with pain you will give birth to children. Your desire will be for your husband, and he will rule over you." To Adam he said, "Because you listened to your wife and ate from the tree about which I commanded you, 'You must not eat of it,' Cursed is the ground because of you; through painful toil you will eat of it all the days of your life. It will produce thorns and thistles for you, and you will eat the plants of the field. By the sweat of your brow you will eat your food until you return to the ground, since from it you were taken; for dust you are and to dust you will return" (Gen. 3:14–19).
Narrator:	The LORD God made garments of skin for Adam and his wife and clothed them. And the LORD God said, "The man has now become like one of us, knowing good and evil" (Gen. 3:21–22a).
Voice of God:	"[Adam] must not be allowed to reach out his hand and take also from the tree of life and eat, and live forever" (Gen. 3:22b).
Narrator:	So the LORD God banished him from the Garden of Eden to work the ground from which he had been taken. After he drove the man out, he placed on the east side of the Garden of Eden cherubim and a flaming sword flashing back and forth to guard the way to the tree of life (Gen. 3:23–24).

Story of Cain and Abel

Narrator: In the story of Cain and Abel we see violence with man against man for the first time.

Narrator: Now Abel kept flocks, and Cain worked the soil. In the course of time Cain brought some of the fruits of the soil as an offering to the LORD. But Abel brought fat portions from some of the firstborn of his flock. The LORD looked with favor on Abel and his offering, but on Cain and his offering he did not look with favor. So Cain was very angry, and his face was downcast (Gen. 4:2b–5).

Voice of God: "Cain, why are you angry? Why is your face downcast? If you do what is right, will you not be accepted? But if you do not do what is right, sin is crouching at your door; it desires to have you, but you must master it" (Gen. 4:6–7).

Cain doesn't answer God but turns and speaks to Abel.

Cain: "Abel, let's go out to the field."

Cain and Abel walk to a different part of the stage where Cain picks up a club and pretends to kill Abel. He then walks back to the point where he last spoke to God.

Voice of God: "Where is your brother Abel?" (Gen. 4:9a).

Cain: "I don't know. Am I my brother's keeper?" (Gen. 4:9b).

Voice of God: "What have you done? Listen! Your brother's blood cries out to me from the

	ground. Now you are under a curse and driven from the ground, which opened its mouth to receive your brother's blood from your hand. When you work the ground, it will no longer yield its crops for you. You will be a restless wanderer on the earth" (Gen. 4:10–12).
Cain:	"My punishment is more than I can bear. Today you are driving me from the land, and I will be hidden from your presence; I will be a restless wanderer on the earth, and whoever finds me will kill me" (Gen. 4:13–14).
Voice of God:	"Not so; if anyone kills [you], he will suffer vengeance seven times over." Then the LORD put a mark on Cain so that no one who found him would kill him. So Cain went out from the LORD's presence and lived in the land of Nod, east of Eden (Gen. 4:15b–16).

Looking for Peace

Narrator:	Throughout the Old Testament we discover conflicts and war between nations and peoples. God offers peace in a world of pain. If only we, his people, would listen.
Speaker 1:	"If you follow my decrees and are careful to obey my commands, I will send you rain in its season, and the ground will yield its crops and the trees of the field their fruit. Your threshing will continue until grape harvest and the grape harvest will continue until planting, and you will eat all the food you want and live in safety in your land" (Lev. 26:3–6).

Speaker 2: I will lie down and sleep in peace, for you alone, O Lord, make me dwell in safety (Ps. 4:8).

Speaker 3: The Lord gives strength to his people; the Lord blesses his people with peace (Ps. 29:11).

Speaker 4: I will listen to what God the Lord will say; he promises peace to his people, his saints—but let them not return to folly. Surely his salvation is near those who fear him, that his glory may dwell in our land. Love and faithfulness meet together; righteousness and peace kiss each other (Ps. 85:8–10).

Speaker 5: There is deceit in the hearts of those who plot evil, but joy for those who promote peace (Prov. 12:20).

Speaker 6: A heart at peace gives life to the body, but envy rots the bones (Prov. 14:30).

Speaker 7: When a man's ways are pleasing to the Lord, he makes even his enemies live at peace with him (Prov. 16:7).

Speaker 8: A time to love and a time to hate, a time for war and a time for peace (Eccles. 3:8).

Speaker 9: "Your sons hasten back, and those who laid you waste depart from you. Lift up your eyes and look around; all your sons gather and come to you. As surely as I live," declares the Lord, "you will wear them all as ornaments; you will put them on, like a bride" (Isa. 49:17–18).

Speaker 10: How beautiful on the mountains are the feet of those who bring good news, who proclaim peace, who bring good

	tidings, who proclaim salvation, who say to Zion, "Your God reigns!" (Isa. 52:7).
Speaker 11:	Those who walk uprightly enter into peace; they find rest as they lie in death (Isa. 57:2).
Speaker 12:	"There is no peace," says my God, "for the wicked" (Isa. 57:21).
Narrator:	Man's search for peace would be hopeless had God not intervened. The prophet Isaiah tells us what the hope of a Messiah would bring.
Child 1:	For to us a child is born, to us a son is given, and the government will be on his shoulders.
Child 2:	And he will be called Wonderful Counselor, Mighty God, Everlasting Father, Prince of Peace.
Child 3:	Of the increase of his government and peace there will be no end.
Child 4:	He will reign on David's throne and over his kingdom, establishing and upholding it with justice and righteousness from that time on and forever. The zeal of the Lord Almighty will accomplish this (Isa. 9:6–7).
Narrator:	Jesus was born of a virgin named Mary. He lived only thirty-three years, but the truths he taught will be with us forever. The Jews misunderstood the purpose of the Messiah. The Romans saw him as a threat to peace. But no one else could bring such peace into the world.

Birth of Jesus

Song by Sunday
school: "While Shepherds Watched Their Flocks by Night"

Several children dressed as sheep enter the stage area with the shepherds. The children are playing among the sheep. The shepherds are making supper over a camp fire.

Narrator: The Bible tells us in Luke 2:8 that "there were shepherds living out in the fields nearby, keeping watch over their flocks at night." Let's listen to their conversation.

Shepherd 1: Come over here to eat now, children. Supper is ready.

Shepherd 2: It's a long night, children, so eat well and clean your plates.

Child 1: Dad, I am happy you let us help you tonight.

Shepherd 1: Since Jacob is sick we need extra help tonight watching his sheep.

Child 2: Tell us what happens at night. Do wolves ever come to steal the sheep from us?

Shepherd 2: Not very often, but we need to make sure. The bigger problem is keeping the sheep near us and not letting them wander away.

Shepherd 1: I remember one night last year when a wolf tried to steal one of the lambs.

Children: Tell us about it. Yes, please tell us!

Shepherd 1: It was the night of the feast of the Passover when a hungry wolf decided to break in by our sheep. Zack was on

	duty to watch the sheep on the north ridge. It was about midnight; we were all relaxing by the fire almost like we are now, when suddenly he blew his horn. It scared me half to death. Shepherds never blow their horns at night unless something is really wrong. We went running over to the ridge. There was Zack, rolling and rolling on the ground with the biggest, the meanest, the ugliest wolf I have ever seen. Its teeth were larger than my arm. The wolf's mouth was so big he could have swallowed Zack with just one bite.
Shepherd 2:	Now, John, just tell the story as it really happened. Don't scare the children.
Shepherd 1:	Well anyway, here was Zack rolling on the ground with it when it broke free. That big, mean, ugly . . . .
Shepherd 2:	John!
Shepherd 1:	Okay, the wolf broke free, grabbed one of the lambs and started to run off. Just then Zack took his staff, hooked the wolf's neck with the curved end, and with one mighty pull he broke the neck of the big, mean, ugly, old wolf. We took the lamb in our arms and carried it back to camp. A couple of weeks later the lamb was bouncing along with the other lambs again.
Children:	That was a good story. Please tell us another one.
Shepherd 2:	Maybe after dinner. Now clean your plates.
Narrator:	Luke 2:9 tells us "an angel of the Lord

appeared to them, and the glory of the Lord shone around them, and they were terrified."

An angel enters the shepherds' camp. The shepherds appear to be very afraid.

Shepherd 1: What is that???

Children: We're afraid. Dad, tell it to go away. He's after us, Help!!!

Shepherd 1: Amos, come quick; Bring your staff and slingshot.

Shepherd 2 comes with a staff and slingshot.

Shepherd 2: Get away from our sheep!!!

Then the angel says:

Angel 1: "Do not be afraid. I bring you good tidings of great joy that will be for all the people. Today in the town of David a Savior has been born to you; he is Christ the Lord. This will be a sign to you: You will find a baby wrapped in cloths and lying in a manger" (Luke 2:10b–12).

Narrator: Suddenly a great company of the heavenly host appeared with the angel praising God and saying, (Luke 2:13):

Four or five other angels join the first angel and say together:

Angel Host: "Glory to God in the highest, and on earth peace to men on whom his favor rests" (Luke 2:14).

Angels leave.

Shepherd 1: I have never seen anything like that before.

Children: Daddy, we're still scared. Who were they?

Shepherd 1: Those were angels, children. They were here to tell us about a very special event.

Shepherd 2: "Let's go to Bethlehem and see this thing that has happened, which the Lord has told us about" (Luke 2:15b).

The shepherds leave the stage. The stage is reset for the stable and manger scene while the children sing.

Songs by
Sunday school: "Angels from the Realms of Glory," "Hark! the Herald Angels Sing," and "Silent Night"

Mary and Joseph enter and sit near the manger. The shepherds enter when the narrator begins speaking.

Narrator: [The shepherds] hurried off and found Mary and Joseph, and the baby, who was lying in the manger. When they had seen him, they spread the word concerning what had been told them about this child, and all who had heard it were amazed at what the shepherds said to them. But Mary treasured up all these things and pondered them in her heart. The shepherds returned, glorifying and praising God for all the things they had heard and seen, which were just as they had been told (Luke 2:16–20).

	At this time the offering for our church's mission projects will be received.
Offering	*During the offering the stage is cleared for the next skit.*
Narrator:	Please stand and sing all the verses of "What Child Is This?"
Congregational Song:	"What Child Is This?"

Jesus Brings Peace

Two children stand on stage discussing the purpose of Jesus' Coming to the world.

Matthew:	"My dad says the Messiah who comes will bring peace to the world."
John:	"No, he won't, Matt. The Messiah is going to conquer the Romans through war. He will show them a thing or two. My dad said so!" (He begins to play fight with a knife or a sword).
Voice of God:	"I will make a covenant of peace with them; it will be an everlasting covenant. I will establish them and increase their numbers, and I will put my sanctuary among them forever" (Ezek. 37:26).
Matthew:	"Did you hear that?"
John:	"No." (He goes on play fighting).
Voice of God:	"I will take away the chariots from Ephraim and the war-horses from Jerusalem, and the battle bow will be broken. He will proclaim peace to the nations. His rule will extend from sea to

	sea and from the River to the ends of the earth" (Zech. 9:10).
Matthew:	"There it is again. The Voice. Did you hear it?"
John:	"The only thing I hear is the sound of my sword conquering the Romans." (continues to play fight)

A man dressed as Jesus enters; many children are gathered around him. Careful not to show his face, he sits with his back to the audience and tenderly speaks with the children. Some of the children can be sitting on his lap and some kneeling by his side. There will also be three men dressed as disciples listening to Jesus speak.
As he speaks Matt and John join the other children.

Voice of Jesus:	"And if anyone causes one of these little ones who believe in me to sin, it would be better for him to be thrown into the sea with a large millstone tied around his neck." My precious little ones, listen to what I have to say, "Blessed are the poor in spirit, for theirs is the kingdom of heaven. Blessed are those who mourn, for they will be comforted. Blessed are the meek, for they will inherit the earth. Blessed are those who hunger and thirst for righteousness, for they will be filled. Blessed are the merciful, for they will be shown mercy. Blessed are the pure in heart, for they will see God. Blessed are the peacemakers, for they will be called sons of God. Blessed are those who are persecuted because of righteousness, for theirs is the kingdom of heaven. Do not let your hearts be troubled. Trust in God; trust also in me. In my Father's house are many rooms; if it were not so, I

	would have told you. I am going there to prepare a place for you. And if I go and prepare a place for you, I will come back and take you to be with me that you also may be where I am. You know the way to the place where I am going" (Mark 9:42, Matt. 5:3–10, John 14:1–4).
Thomas:	"Lord, we don't know where you are going, so how can we know the way?" (John 14:5).
Voice of Jesus:	"I am the way and the truth and the life. No one comes to the Father except through me. If you really knew me, you would know my Father as well. From now on, you do know him and have seen him. I tell you the truth, anyone who has faith in me will do what I have been doing. He will do even greater things than these, because I am going to the Father. And I will do whatever you ask in my name, so that the Son may bring glory to the Father. You may ask me for anything in my name, and I will do it. All this I have spoken while still with you. But the Counselor, the Holy Spirit, whom the Father will send in my name, will teach you all things and will remind you of everything I have said to you. Peace I leave with you; my peace I give you. I do not give to you as the world gives. Do not let your hearts be troubled and do not be afraid. I have told you these things, so that in me you may have peace. In this world you will have trouble. But take heart! I have overcome the world" (John 14:6–7, 12–14, 25–27, John 16:33).

Clear the stage for the pastor's message.

The Message

The message from Acts 10:34–43 is brought by the pastor (or some other capable person).

Peter: My name is Peter. I am happy to come and speak with your congregation. The message I bring you today is just as relevant as when I first spoke it at the time of the New Testament church. "I now realize how true it is that God does not show favoritism but accepts men from every nation who fear him and do what is right. This is the message God sent to the people of Israel, telling the good news of peace through Jesus Christ, who is Lord of all. You know what has happened throughout Judea, beginning in Galilee after the baptism that John preached—how God anointed Jesus of Nazareth with the Holy Spirit and power, and how he went around doing good and healing all who were under the power of the devil, because God was with him. We are witnesses of everything he did in the country of the Jews and in Jerusalem. They killed him by hanging him on a tree, but God raised him from the dead on the third day and caused him to be seen. He was not seen by all the people, but by witnesses whom God had already chosen—by us who ate and drank with him after he rose from the dead. He commanded us to preach to the people and to testify that he is the one whom God appointed as judge of the living and the dead. All the prophets testify about him that everyone who believes in him receives forgiveness of sins through his name" (Acts 10:34b–43).

We look for peace and order in our lives by establishing: *secure jobs*—in a time when layoffs and change of job status are prevalent; *secure family structure*—when divorce occurs in almost one out of every two families; *educational facilities and governments to teach us truth*—when some teach that man has come to the world through evolution and our nation has legalized abortion.

Peace can come only when one establishes a relationship with the living Prince of Peace, King Jesus. We need to stop carrying our own burdens and let Jesus justify our lives before God. Then we can say with the apostle Paul in Romans 5:1:

Speaker 1: Therefore, since we have been justified through faith, we have peace with God through our Lord Jesus Christ.

Peter: Believe this the gospel of Jesus, and live.

Peter exits.

Pastor: Please make additions or deletions in the message to fit your style and congregation.

*Song by congregation:	"Jesus Is All the World to Me" (or another song to fit the theme of the message).
Song by Sunday school:	"I've Got Peace Like a River"

*Congregation Standing

Promises of Peace

Narrator:	God promises us peace when we follow his path. The children have a few passages relating to these promises.
Child 1:	The mind of sinful man is death, but the mind controlled by the Spirit is life and peace (Rom. 8:6).
Child 2:	For the kingdom of God is not a matter of eating and drinking, but of righteousness, peace and joy in the Holy Spirit. Let us therefore make every effort to do what leads to peace and to mutual edification (Rom. 14:17, 19).
Child 3:	For God is not a God of disorder but of peace (1 Cor. 14:33a).
Child 4:	But the fruit of the Spirit is love, joy, peace, patience, kindness, goodness, faithfulness, gentleness and self-control. Against such things there is no law (Gal. 5:22–23).
Child 5:	But now in Christ Jesus you who once were far away have been brought near through the blood of Christ. For he himself is our peace, who has made the two one and has destroyed the barrier, the dividing wall of hostility . . . (Eph. 2:13–14).

Child 6: His purpose was to create in himself one new man out of the two, thus making peace, and in this one body to reconcile both of them to God through the cross, by which he put to death their hostility (Eph. 2:15b–16).

Child 7: He came and preached peace to you who were far away and peace to those who were near (Eph. 2:17).

Child 8: Do not be anxious about anything, but in everything, by prayer and petition, with thanksgiving, present your requests to God. And the peace of God, which transcends all understanding, will guard your hearts and your minds in Christ Jesus (Phil. 4:6–7).

Child 9: Finally, brothers, whatever is true, whatever is noble, whatever is right, whatever is pure, whatever is lovely, whatever is admirable—if anything is excellent or praiseworthy—think about such things (Phil. 4:8).

Child 10: Let the peace of Christ rule in your hearts, since as members of one body you were called to peace. And be thankful (Col. 3:15).

Child 11: Make every effort to live in peace with all men and to be holy; without holiness no one will see the Lord (Heb. 12:14).

Child 12: But the wisdom that comes from heaven is first of all pure; then peace loving, considerate, submissive, full of mercy and good fruit, impartial and sincere. Peacemakers who sow in peace raise a harvest of righteousness (James 3:17–18).

Solo: "It Is Well With My Soul" sung by a member of the congregation.

Closing

Narrator: The children today began by speaking of war but Jesus shows us peace; peace that is strong and firm. It is only through a personal relationship with God that true peace is found in our hearts and lives. Thank you, children, for bringing this message of peace from Jesus who is the King of Kings, the eternal Lord of Lords, the everlasting Prince of Peace.

The children distribute flowers to the congregation during the song "Meaning of Love."

Closing song: Play from tape (or person may sing) the "Meaning of Love" by Farell and Farell.

Narrator: Please rise for the benediction.

Finally, brothers, good-by. Aim for perfection, listen to my appeal, be of one mind, live in peace. And the God of love and peace will be with you (2 Cor. 13:11).

Organ Postlude

5

The Light of Jesus

Notes to the Director

The program focuses on LIGHT. Each class will enter from the back of the church, led by the teacher who carries an oil-burning lamp. All sanctuary lights are to be out; the oil lamps alone give light. The children are to be singing "Give Me Oil in My Lamp" while entering. This should be practiced a few times so the children get used to singing and walking in the dark.

Each child should bring a flashlight to shine when singing "This Little Light of Mine."

The songs "Thy Word" and "No Room" can either be sung by a soloist or played through the sound system on cassette tape.

The part of Paul is usually played by the pastor or an individual who is able to communicate well in public. The lines need not be completely memorized; however, the person playing the role should be thoroughly familiar with the content.

The closing of the program will require placing battery-operated candles in each pew.

List of Characters

Introduction to the program

Narrator 1
Narrator 2
Speakers 1–12 (three- through five-year-olds)
Speakers A–C (fifth graders)

Old Testament Psalms

Speakers 1–14 (first through third graders)

Transition to the New Testament

Speaker 1 (fifth grader)

New Testament Skit

Gabriel (fourth grader)
Mary (fourth grader)
Joseph (fourth grader)
Simeon (fourth grader)

Life of Jesus

Speakers 1–5 (fourth graders)

Challenge for Today

King Agrippa (adult)
Paul (Pastor or adult)

Closing

Speakers 1–8 (first through third graders)

Songs

Give Me Oil in My Lamp
Welcome Song

This Little Light of Mine
Jesus Loves Me
Jesus Loves the Little Children
Heavenly Sunshine
Thy Word
The Light of the World Is Jesus
For God So Loved the World
Silent Night! Holy Night!
It Came Upon the Midnight Clear
No Room
Away in a Manger
Angels We Have Heard on High
I'll Be a Sunbeam for Jesus
Sunshine in My Heart
Pass It On

Props

Introduction

Flashlight for each child
Oil lamp for each teacher

Old Testament Psalms

Card with printed verse of Scripture for each of the Psalm speakers

New Testament Skit

Old Testament costumes for Mary, Joseph, and Simeon may be made from old robes, striped material, sheets, etc. Sandals should be worn.

Angel Gabriel should be dressed in a white robe made from material or a sheet. Halo and wings should be worn.

A setting of a house will be required for the scene with Mary and Gabriel.

Challenge for Today

New Testament costume for Paul can be made from old robes, striped material, or sheets. Sandals should be worn.

King Agrippa should be wearing a royal robe and a crown; he will also need a throne.

Closing

Each congregational member should be provided with a battery-operated candle.

—The Light of Jesus—

Introduction to the Program

Begin with the auditorium dark. When "Let there be light" is said, turn on a spotlight to illuminate the front of church. Next, have the children enter from the back of church marching and singing "Give Me Oil in My Lamp." Each teacher carries a lit, oil-burning lamp while leading his or her class in. Only the spotlight and the teachers' lamps should be on. After all the children are in, turn on the house lights.

Narrator 2: In the beginning God created the heavens and the earth. Now the earth was formless and empty, darkness was over the surface of the deep, and the Spirit of God was hovering over the waters. And God said "Let there be light," and there was light. God saw that the light was good, and he separated the light from the darkness. God called the light "day" and the darkness he called "night." And there was evening, and there was morning—the first day (Gen. 1:1–5).

Narrator: Welcome to our program. We are here to celebrate Jesus' birthday. The children have just sung "Give Me Oil in My Lamp." We are going to focus on how God as our lamp and light will light our paths.

Welcome

Song by Primary Department—"Welcome Song"

Three- through five-year-old speaker
Speaker 1   This little light of mine,

Three- through five-year-old speaker
Speaker 2   I'm going to let it shine,

Three- through five-year-old speaker
Speaker 3   This little light of mine,

Three- through five-year-old speaker
Speaker 4   I'm going to let it shine,

Fifth grade speaker from the back corner of church
Speaker A   Let it shine,

Fifth grade speaker from another back corner of church
Speaker B   Let it shine,

Fifth grade speaker from the center isle in the middle of church
Speaker C   Let it shine.

The fifth grade speakers hold flashlights and shine them all over the people, ceiling, and walls while they speak.

Three- through five-year-old speaker
Speaker 5   Don't let Satan blow it out,

Three- through five-year-old speaker
Speaker 6   I'm going to let it shine,

Three- through five-year-old speaker
Speaker 7   Don't let Satan blow it out,

Three- through five-year-old speaker
Speaker 8   I'm going to let it shine,

Fifth grade speaker from the back corner of church
Speaker A   Let it shine,

Fifth grade speaker from another back corner of church
Speaker B   Let it shine,

Fifth grade speaker from the center isle in the middle of church
Speaker C   Let it shine.

Three- through five-year-old speaker
Speaker 9   Let it shine till Jesus comes,

Three- through five-year-old speaker
Speaker 10   I'm going to let it shine,

Three- through five-year-old speaker
Speaker 11   Let it shine till Jesus comes,

Three- through five-year-old speaker
Speaker 12   I'm going to let it shine,

Fifth grade speaker from the back corner of church
Speaker A   Let it shine,

Fifth grade speaker from another back corner of church

Speaker B   Let it shine,

Fifth grade speaker from the center isle in the middle of church

Speaker C   Let it shine.

The entire Sunday school (Three-year-olds through fifth graders) turn on their flashlights and sing "This Little Light of Mine."

Narrator: You are the light of the world. A city on a hill cannot be hidden. Neither do people light a lamp and put it under a bowl. Instead they put it on its stand, and it gives light to everyone in the house (Matt. 5:14–15). In the same way, let your light shine before men, that they may see your good deeds and praise your Father in heaven (Matt. 5:16).

Songs by primary children—"Jesus Loves Me" and "Jesus Loves the Little Children"

Old Testament Psalms

Narrator: God often spoke to his people through Old Testament writers, comparing himself to a light. When God led the Israelites from captivity under the Egyptian rule of Pharaoh, he led them through the desert by day with a pillar of smoke and at night with a pillar of fire. The Psalms are full of verses speaking of the light God gives.

Listen as our children share some of these with us.

First through Third Grades

Speaker 1: Psalm 4:6—Many are asking, "Who can show us any good?" Let the light of your face shine upon us, O LORD.

Speaker 2: Psalm 13:3—Look on me and answer, O LORD my God. Give light to my eyes, or I will sleep in death.

Speaker 3: Psalm 18:28—You, O LORD, keep my lamp burning; my God turns my darkness into light.

Song by Sunday school: "Heavenly Sunshine"

Speaker 4: Psalm 19:8—The precepts of the LORD are right, giving joy to the heart. The commands of the LORD are radiant, giving light to the eyes.

Speaker 5: Psalm 27:1a—The LORD is my light and my salvation–whom shall I fear?

Speaker 6: Psalm 36:9—For with you is the fountain of life; in your light we see light.

Speaker 7: Psalm 43:3—Send forth your light and your truth, let them guide me; let them bring me to your holy mountain, to the place where you dwell.

Speaker 8: Psalm 89:15—Blessed are those who have learned to acclaim you, who walk in the light of your presence, O LORD.

Speaker 9: Psalm 104:1–2a—Praise the LORD, O my soul. O LORD my God, you are very great; you are clothed with splendor and majesty. He wraps himself in light as with a garment.

Speaker 10: Psalm 112:4—Even in darkness light dawns for the upright, for the gracious and compassionate and righteous man.

Speaker 11: Psalm 118:27a—The LORD is God, and he has made his light shine upon us.

Speaker 12: Psalm 119:105—Your word is a lamp to my feet and a light for my path.

Speaker 13: Psalm 119:130—The entrance of your words gives light; it gives understanding to the simple.

Speaker 14: Psalm 139:12—Even the darkness will not be dark to you; the night will shine like the day, for darkness is as light to you.

Song: "Thy Word"—by Amy Grant

This song may either be sung by a member in the church or played from Amy Grant's tape.

Narrator: People of God, this song by Amy Grant shows us if we follow the path God has set for us there is nothing we need to fear because God offers a source of everlasting truth. This truth is shown in the birth and life of his only son Jesus.

Please join the children in the song "The Light of the World Is Jesus." Remain seated during the singing of this song while the offering is received.

Congregation sings: "The Light of the World Is Jesus"

Offering: To be taken during the singing of "The Light of the World Is Jesus"

Transition to the New Testament

The following verses may be said by children (if there are enough children in the Sunday school) or Narrator 2.

Narrator 2: "For God so loved the world that he gave his one and only Son, that whoever believes in him shall not perish but have eternal life. For God did not send his Son into the world to condemn the world, but to save the world through him. Whoever believes in him is not condemned, but whoever does not believe stands condemned already because he has not believed in the name of God's one and only Son. This is the verdict: Light has come into the world, but men loved darkness instead of light because their deeds were evil. Everyone who does evil hates the light, and will not come into the light for fear that his deeds will be exposed. But whoever lives by the truth comes into the light, so that it may be seen plainly that what he has done has been done through God" (John 3:16–21).

Songs by Sunday school: "For God So Loved the World," "Silent Night" and "It Came Upon the Midnight Clear"

New Testament Skit

Start this part of the program with the lights off again. As the reading progresses, turn up the lights.

Narrator 2: In the beginning was the Word, and

the Word was with God, and the Word was God. He was with God in the beginning. Through him all things were made; without him nothing was made that has been made. In him was life, and that life was the light of men. The light shines in the darkness, but the darkness has not understood it. There came a man who was sent from God; his name was John. He came as a witness to testify concerning that light, so that through him all men might believe. He himself was not the light; he came only as a witness to the light. The true light that gives light to every man was coming into the world (John 1:1–9). The Word became flesh and lived for a while among us. We have seen his glory, the glory of the one and only Son, who came from the Father, full of grace and truth (John 1:14).

Narrator 2: In the sixth month, God sent the angel Gabriel to Nazareth, a town in Galilee, to a virgin pledged to be married to a man named Joseph, a descendant of David. The virgin's name was Mary (Luke 1:26–27).

Mary enters and sits in a chair. An angel comes and talks with Mary. She stands when the angel speaks to her.

Narrator 2: The angel went to her and said,
Gabriel: "Greetings, you who are highly favored! The Lord is with you." (Luke 1:28).
Mary: Who are you? What are you doing in my house?

Gabriel:	"Do not be afraid, Mary, you have found favor with God. You will be with child and give birth to a son, and you are to give him the name Jesus. He will be great and will be called the Son of the Most High. The Lord God will give him the throne of his father David, and he will reign over the house of Jacob forever; his kingdom will never end" (Luke 1:30–33).
Narrator:	Mary and Joseph did have a son. She named him Jesus as the angel Gabriel had told her. Jesus wasn't born in a nice hospital as babies are today; rather, Jesus was born in a place where sheep, goats, cows, and donkeys live. Joseph tried to find room for his wife in an inn, but there was no room there. God's only Son had a humble beginning in a manger.
Song:	"No Room"—sung by a soloist
Narrator:	Let's listen to the children tell of Jesus' birth through song.
Songs by Sunday school children:	"Away in a Manger" and "Angels We Have Heard on High"

Set up the temple scene. Have Mary and Joseph ready to go to temple as the narrator reads.

Narrator:	Joseph and Mary brought Jesus to the temple to be circumcised according to the law. At the temple an old man named Simeon was waiting. God had told him through the Holy Spirit that he would not die until he had seen the Lord's Christ. Listen to Simeon:

Mary, Joseph, and baby Jesus stand near Simeon and listen to Simeon as if he is speaking.

Narrator 2: "Sovereign Lord, as you have promised, you now dismiss your servant in peace. For my eyes have seen your salvation, which you have prepared in the sight of all people, a light for revelation to the Gentiles and for glory to your people Israel" (Luke 2:27–32).

Children are seated; the stage is cleared.

Narrator: And the child Jesus grew and became strong; he was filled with wisdom, and the grace of God was upon him (Luke 2:40).

Life of Jesus

Narrator: Jesus' teachings have been recorded by the apostles in the New Testament.

Speaker 1: "I am the light of the world. Whoever follows me will never walk in darkness, but will have the light of life" (John 8:12).

Speaker 2: "While I am in the world, I am the light of the world" (John 9:5).

Speaker 3: "You are going to have the light just a little while longer. Walk while you have the light, before darkness overtakes you" (John 12:35a).

Speaker 4: "The man who walks in the dark does not know where he is going. Put your trust in the light while you have it, so that you may become sons of light" (John 12:35b–36a).

Speaker 5: "I have come into the world as a light, so that no one who believes in me should stay in darkness" (John 12:46).

Narrator: God sent Jesus into the world to live a perfect life. Jesus' life was full of examples for us to follow. Jesus showed us that he is the only way, truth, and life. If we believe on him, we will not perish but live with God forever. After Jesus rose from the dead he appeared to many people before going to heaven to live with God. He is preparing a place for those who believe in him as well. The questions we need to ask ourselves this Christmas are: "Does Jesus live in my life? Is his lifestyle shown by the way I conduct my house, by the way I communicate with others, by the way I show love to friends, children, and spouses?" The apostle Paul was converted to believe in Jesus on the road to Damascus. In defense of the Christian faith Paul gave this testimony to King Agrippa. Let's listen as he tells the story:

Challenge for Today

Paul may be portrayed by the pastor or another adult. King Agrippa is sitting on a throne.

Paul: "King Agrippa, I consider myself fortunate to stand before you today as I make my defense against all accusations of the Jews, and especially so because you are so well acquainted with all the Jewish customs and controversies. Therefore, I beg you to listen to me patiently. The Jews all know the way I have lived ever since I was a child, from the beginning of my life in my own country, and also in Jerusalem. They have known me for a long time and can testify, if they are willing, that according to the strictest sect of our religion, I have lived as a Pharisee. And now it is because of my hope in what God has promised our fathers that I am on trial today. This is the promise our twelve tribes are hoping to see fulfilled as they earnestly serve God day and night. O king, it is because of this hope that the Jews are accusing me. Why should any of you consider it incredible that God raises the dead? I too was convinced that I ought to do all that was possible to oppose the name of Jesus of Nazareth. And that is just what I did in Jerusalem. On the authority of the chief priests I put many of the saints in prison, and when they were put to death, I cast my vote against them. Many a time I went from one synagogue to another to have them punished, and I tried to force them to blaspheme. In my obsession against them, I even went to foreign cities to persecute them. On one of these journeys I was going to Damascus with the authority and commission of the chief priests. About noon, O king, as I was on the road, I saw a light from heaven, brighter than the sun, blazing around me and my companions. We all fell to the ground, and I heard a voice saying to me in Aramaic, 'Saul, Saul, why do you persecute me? It is hard for you to kick against the goads.' Then I asked, 'Who are you, Lord?' 'I am Jesus, whom you are persecuting,' the Lord replied. 'Now get up and stand on your feet. I have appeared to you to appoint you as a servant and as a witness of what you have seen of me and what I will show you. I will rescue you from your own people and from the Gentiles. I am sending you to open their eyes and turn them from darkness to light, and from the power of Satan to God, so that they may receive forgiveness of sins and a place among those who are sanctified by faith in me'" (Acts 26:2–18).

Paul turns and directs the closing lines only to the congregation.

Have you given your life to Jesus? Have you asked him to be Savior and Lord of your home and life? The children leave us with these thoughts:

Closing

Speaker 1: The god of this age has blinded the minds of unbelievers, so that they cannot see the light of the gospel of the glory of Christ, who is the image of God (2 Cor. 4:4).

Speaker 2: For God, who said, "Let light shine out of darkness," made his light shine in our hearts to give us the light of the knowledge of the glory of God in the face of Christ (2 Cor. 4:6).

Speaker 3:	For you were once darkness, but now you are light in the Lord. Live as children of light (for the fruit of the light consists in all goodness, righteousness and truth) (Eph. 5:8–9).
Songs by Sunday school:	"I'll Be a Sunbeam for Jesus" and "Sunshine in My Heart"
Speaker 4:	This is the message we have heard from him and declare to you: God is light; in him there is no darkness at all (1 John 1:5).
Speaker 5:	If we claim to have fellowship with him yet walk in the darkness, we lie and do not live by the truth (1 John 1:6).
Speaker 6:	But if we walk in the light, as he is in the light, we have fellowship with one another, and the blood of Jesus, his Son, purifies us from all sin (1 John 1:7).
Speaker 7:	Yet I am writing you a new command . . . the darkness is passing, and the true light is already shining (1 John 2:8).
Speaker 8:	Anyone who claims to be in the light but hates his brother is still in the darkness. Whoever loves his brother lives in the light, and there is nothing in him to make him stumble (1 John 2:9–10).
Narrator:	The children have just demonstrated what the Bible says about being God's children of light. Battery-operated candles are placed in a box in each pew. Please take one and pass the rest down your pew. When you get your

candle please stand around the outside of the pews forming a large circle around the sanctuary. We will close with the song "Pass It On." The words are printed in the bulletin. Our challenge to you is to be witnesses in the world around us. Let your lights shine brightly for Jesus. Many people in this world are looking for truth. We have the truth *and* the light to live by in Christ Jesus. The pastor will begin by lighting his candle. The person on his left will then light his or her candle and so on until all the candles are lit. Remember, while we light our candles, please remain standing and sing the song "Pass It On."

Congregation
Sings: "Pass It On"

Closing comments, prayer, and benediction by the pastor.

6

The Lamb

Notes to the Director

Opening

A stuffed lamb

Adults are best used for the narration, except when the script says:
"Child Narrator."

Old Testament Skit

Mary should be dressed in white costume made from a sheet or suitable fabric.

Joseph can be dressed in any multi-colored costume.

Angels need to be dressed in white robes; halos and wings are optional.

Use a child narrator who speaks loudly, clearly, slowly, and expressively.

The shepherds need multi-colored robes, staffs, and sheep.

Life of Jesus Skit

Need a tape or person to sing the song "Worthy Is the Lamb."

Modern Day Skit

The apostle John is best done by an adult with a deep, slow, speaking voice.

The elder should be played by an adult.
The four speakers should be children of any age who can speak well together.

Closing

There is an optional closing offered. Choose one that will fit the theology and traditions of your church.

List of Characters

Opening

Old Testament Shepherd
Several children (carrying presents)

Program Welcome

Three-year-old class

Introduction to the Program

7 speakers (four- and five-year-olds) for the theme "The Lamb"

Old Testament Skit

Narrator (adult)
Child Speakers (numbers 1–4)
Speakers (numbers 1–3)

New Testament Skit

Child Narrator
Angel 1
Mary (nonspeaking role)
Joseph (nonspeaking role)
Shepherds (group of 4–5)
Angel 2
Angels (group of 4–5)

Life of Jesus

Child Narrator 2

Modern Day Skit

Apostle John (adult)
Elder (adult)
Choral Speakers (group of four speakers talk in unison)

Props

Opening

Either make the cross solid enough to hold the lamb or tie the lamb to another piece of furniture near the cross.

Introduction to the Program

The letters for the *Introduction to the Program* can be made of cardboard with pictures on each card of the item represented.

Costumes for various characters are described in the notes to the director.

The stage should be simple with at least two sections that divide different settings.

Songs

Watch the Lamb
The B–I–B–L–E
Jesus Loves the Little Children
This Little Light of Mine
Have You Heard
Noah-Noah
Our God Reigns
While Shepherds Watched Their Flocks by Night
Silent Night! Holy Night!
Angels from the Realms of Glory

Worthy Is the Lamb
Savior, Like a Shepherd Lead Us
Organ Postlude: Worthy Is the Lamb
Shepherd of Love (optional closing)
Gentle Shepherd (optional closing)
Savior, Like a Shepherd Lead Us (optional closing)

Opening

Begin the program with a person dressed as an Old Testament shepherd carrying a lamb up the aisle from the rear of church. The shepherd ties the lamb to a cross made of wood on the stage. Then children bring out wrapped presents and place them around the lamb. The auditorium should be dark with a spotlight only on the lamb, the Old Testament shepherd, and the children.

Play "Watch the Lamb" by Ray Boltz as soon as the shepherd begins to walk down the aisle and continue while the spotlight is on the lamb and the children bring out the presents.

Clear the stage for the *Program Welcome* when the song is done.

Program Welcome—Three-year-olds

Three-year-olds—We may be small and not too tall, but our message is clear, we're happy you're here.
Opening songs—Primary Department
"The B–I–B–L–E" and "Jesus Loves the Little Children"

Introduction to the Program

- **T** is for turning, like lambs, from straying, to pathways of learning.
- **H** is for hill, the place where Jesus died while doing his Father's will.
- **E** is for eternal, the time we are with God and saved from the inferno.

L is for love, the one God sent us from heaven above.

A is for almighty, the God we serve who is so strong and mighty.

M is for mission; we share good news of Jesus to fulfill God's Great Commission.

B is for boat, from which Jesus taught us the difference between sheep and goats.

Songs—Primary Department
"This Little Light of Mine" and "Have You Heard"

*Primary children leave stage and
Old Testament Skit is set up on the stage.*

Old Testament Skit

Narrator: The Bible makes references to many types of animals. In Genesis we read the account of creation. God made animals of all shapes and sizes. Later God saw the corruption man had caused on the earth so he caused a flood. Noah and his family were spared in an ark. Before the rains started, Noah gathered all types of animals together two by two. These animals were spared with Noah and again began to re-populate the earth. Our children would like to sing "Noah-Noah."

Song by Sunday school—"Noah-Noah"

Narrator: Of all the different types of animals in this world God chose one to be special. It represents purity and accounts for the sin man commits. The animal is the lamb. Sheep were and still are a very popular animal in the Jewish social and economical life. To be a shepherd was an honorable profession in the Bible. Genesis 4 tells us the story of Cain and Abel. Cain was a hunter and Abel a shepherd. These are the first two professions recorded in ancient history. King David, who killed Goliath, began as a shepherd boy in the foothills of Israel. One of the Psalms David wrote has become very special to many people. The first grade class will share Psalm 23 with us.

Child 1: The LORD is my shepherd, I shall lack nothing. He makes me lie down in green pastures, he leads me beside quiet waters, he restores my soul. He guides me in paths of righteousness for his name's sake.

Child 2: Even though I walk through the valley of the shadow of death, I will fear no evil, for you are with me; your rod and your staff, they comfort me.

Child 3: You prepare a table before me in the presence of my enemies. You anoint my head with oil; my cup overflows.

Child 4: Surely goodness and love will follow me all the days of my life, and I will dwell in the house of the LORD forever (Ps. 23).

Narrator: You see, people of God, we are all sheep in God's world. Some of us have found the Good Shepherd. Others of us are still looking for a shepherd to lead us beside the quiet, still waters. We hope tonight you will see Jesus not merely as a baby in a manger from a time long ago. We want to show you a shepherd, a Good Shepherd named Jesus, who is still alive and will help lead you to green pastures. There are many shepherds in the world who attempt to offer peace and salvation to those who will follow. God tells us in Ezekiel 34 the judgment which will fall to the false shepherds and leaders who lead others astray. He also tells us what he will do for us as a shepherd. Listen to the second grade class tell us of God, the Good Shepherd of the Old Testament:

Speaker 1: "For this is what the Sovereign LORD says: I myself will search for my sheep and look after them. As a shepherd looks after his scattered flock when he is with them, so will I look after my sheep. I will rescue them from all the places where they were scattered on a day of clouds and darkness" (Ezek. 34:11–12).

Speaker 2: "I will bring them out from the nations and gather them from the countries, and I will bring them into their own land. I will pasture them on the mountains of Israel, in the ravines, and in all the settlements in the land. I myself will tend my sheep and have them lie down, declares the Sovereign LORD" (Ezek. 34:13, 15).

Speaker 3: "I will search for the lost and bring back the strays. I will bind up the injured and strengthen the weak, but the sleek and the strong I will destroy. I will shepherd the flock with justice. You my sheep, the sheep of my pasture, are people, and I am your God, declares the Sovereign LORD" (Ezek. 34:16, 31).

Narrator:	Please stand and join the children in singing "Our God Reigns."
Congregation Sings:	"Our God Reigns"
Narrator:	At this time the deacons will come forward to receive the offering.

Offertory prayer by the deacons

Offering:	Have the organist play a song reflecting the saving majesty of our God.

New Testament Skit

Narrator:	Many years after the days of Ezekiel, God planted a seed inside a young woman named Mary. This is how the birth of Jesus came about:
Child Narrator 1:	His mother Mary was pledged to be married to Joseph, but before they came together, she was found to be with child through the Holy Spirit.

Mary enters and sits in a chair in a house scene. Joseph enters room and looks at Mary from a distance.

Joseph wasn't sure he should marry Mary because he didn't know the baby was of God. So an angel came and spoke to Joseph and told him:

Angel 1 enters, raises arms and says:

Angel 1:	"Joseph son of David, do not be afraid to take Mary home as your wife, because what is conceived in her is from the Holy Spirit. She will give birth to a son, and you are to give him the

name Jesus, because he will save his people from their sins" (Matt. 1:20b–21).

Angel leaves and Joseph walks over to Mary.

Child Narrator 1: In those days Caesar Augustus issued a decree that a census should be taken of the entire Roman world. (This was the first census that took place while Quirinius was governor of Syria.) And everyone went to his own town to register.

Joseph and Mary leave the house setting and travel down the church aisle to the back of church and then return to the front of church again. While they travel to the rear of church have a spotlight on them. Also, reset the stage with the manger setting.

So Joseph also went up from the town of Nazareth in Galilee to Judea, to Bethlehem the town of David, because he belonged to the house and line of David.

Pause to allow time for Joseph and Mary to travel down and up the aisle.

He went there to register with Mary, who was pledged to be married to him and was expecting a child. While they were there, the time came for the baby to be born, and she gave birth to her first-born, a son. She wrapped him in cloths and placed him in a manger, because there was no room for them in the inn (Luke 2:1–7).

Narrator: The Bible tells us God sent angels to tell of Jesus' birth. These angels didn't go to the king, or to doctors, or even to the priests or Levites; rather, they

	went to tell a few shepherds who were watching sheep in the fields at night, that Jesus had been born in a manger.
Children sing:	"While Shepherds Watched Their Flocks by Night," "Silent Night! Holy Night!" and "Angels from the Realms of Glory"

Set up for shepherd setting. Four or five shepherds enter stage, and Mary and Joseph go to the manger.

Child Narrator 1: And there were shepherds living out in the fields nearby, keeping watch over their flocks at night. An angel of the Lord appeared to them, and the glory of the Lord shone around them, and they were terrified. But the angel said to them,

Angel 2 enters and speaks to shepherds.

Angel 2: "Do not be afraid. I bring you good news of great joy that will be for all the people. Today in the town of David a Savior has been born to you; he is Christ the Lord. This will be a sign to you: You will find a baby wrapped in cloths and lying in a manger."

Child Narrator 1: Suddenly a great company of the heavenly host appeared with the angel, praising God and saying,

Other angels (four or five) join Angel 2 and speak in unison.

Angels all together: "Glory to God in the highest, and on earth peace to men on whom his favor rests."

All angels leave the stage.

Child Narrator 1: When the angels had left them and gone into heaven, the shepherds said to one another,

The shepherds need to be able to speak clearly, loudly, and slowly.

Shepherds: "Let's go to Bethlehem and see this thing that has happened, which the Lord has told us about."

The shepherds leave and walk over to the manger setting near Mary and Joseph.

Child Narrator 1: So they hurried off and found Mary and Joseph, and the baby, who was lying in the manger. When they had seen him, they spread the word concerning what had been told them about this child, and all who heard it were amazed at what the shepherds said to them. But Mary treasured up all these things and pondered them in her heart. The shepherds returned, glorifying and praising God for all the things they had heard and seen, which were just as they had been told (Luke 2:8–20).

Life of Jesus

Narrator: Jesus' life portrayed a perfect example of what the term shepherd means. In John 10 Jesus tells us:

Child Narrator 2: "I am the good shepherd. The good shepherd lays down his life for the sheep. I am the good shepherd; I know my sheep and my sheep know me—just as the Father knows me and I know the Father—and I lay down my life for the sheep. I have other sheep that are not of this sheep pen. I must bring them also. They too will listen to my voice, and there shall be one flock and one shepherd. The reason my Father loves me is that I lay down my life—only to take it up again. No one takes it from me, but I lay it down of my own accord. I have authority to lay it down and authority to take it up again. This command I received from my Father" (John 10:11, 14–18). "My sheep listen to my voice; I know them, and they follow me. I give them eternal life, and they shall never perish; no one can snatch them out of my hand. My Father, who has given them to me, is greater than all; no one can snatch them out of my Father's hand. I and the Father are one" (John 10:27–30).

Narrator: Jesus' life was perfect. He showed us what it is to live to God's glory. He was misunderstood by the leaders of his day. They crucified him on the cross. But just as Jesus had predicted before his death, he rose from the dead on the third day. He now reigns at God's right hand. Some day he will come again and judge between the good and the bad, the sheep and the goats.

Song: "Worthy Is the Lamb"—A tape can be played or the choir or an individual can sing it.

Modern Day Skit

Narrator: We end the program with these words from my friends. The author John portrays a vision from God of heaven and the future of his people. If you are a lamb who is not yet following Jesus, please listen to what the future holds.

Apostle John: Then I saw in the right hand of him who sat on the throne a scroll with writing on both sides and sealed with seven seals. And I saw a mighty angel proclaiming in a loud voice, "Who is worthy to break the seals and open the scroll?" But no one in heaven or on earth or under the earth could open the scroll or even look inside it. I wept and wept because no one could look inside. Then one of the elders said to me,

Elder: "Do not weep! See, the Lion of the tribe of Judah, the Root of David, has triumphed. He is able to open the scroll and its seven seals."

Apostle John: Then I saw a Lamb, looking as if it had been slain, standing in the center of the throne, encircled by the four living creatures and the elders. . . . He came and took the scroll from the right hand of him who sat on the throne. . . . And the four living creatures . . . sang a new song:

Four speakers say in unison: "You are worthy to take the scroll and to open its seals, because you were slain, and with your blood you purchased men for God from every tribe and lan-

	guage and people and nation. You have made them to be a kingdom and priests to serve our God, and they will reign on the earth."
Apostle John:	Then I looked and heard the voice of many angels, numbering thousands upon thousands, and ten thousand times ten thousand. . . . They sang "Worthy is the Lamb, who was slain, to receive power and wealth and wisdom and strength and honor and glory and praise!" Then I heard every creature in heaven and on earth and under the earth and on the sea, and all that is in them, singing: "To him who sits on the throne and to the Lamb be praise and honor and glory and power, for ever and ever!" (Rev. 5:1-13).
Narrator:	The apostle John goes on to explain that those who believe on him will someday live in heaven. Toward the end of Revelation John gives us a glimpse of the heavenly city in the life to come. It will be perfect with no more need for earthly leaders, churches, or temples.
Apostle John:	I did not see a temple in the city, because the Lord God Almighty and the Lamb are its temple. The city does not need the sun or the moon to shine on it, for the glory of God gives it light, and the Lamb is its lamp. The nations will walk by its light, and the kings of the earth will bring their splendor into it. On no day will its gates ever be shut, for there will be no night there (Rev. 21:22-25). Nothing impure will ever enter it, nor will any-

one who does what is shameful or deceitful, but only those whose names are written in the Lamb's book of life (Rev. 21:27). "I, Jesus, have sent my angel to give you this testimony for the churches. I am the Root and the Offspring of David, and the bright Morning Star." The Spirit and the bride say, "Come!" And let him who hears say, "Come!" Whoever is thirsty, let him take the free gift of the water of life (Rev. 22:16–17).

Closing

Narrator: If you have never given your life to Jesus, I invite you to do so tonight. Jesus is the only way to life, truth, and happiness. There are many other shepherds in the world who would lead you astray. Jesus is the Good Shepherd. His paths are straight and true. Please don't leave until you have set your path straight with God. Our pastor and/or elders are available to help you. Please see one of us. Our closing song is "Savior, Like a Shepherd Lead Us." Please stand and sing all the verses.

Congregation Sings: "Savior, Like a Shepherd Lead Us"

While the song is being sung reset the stage with the cross and the lamb.

Pastor: Closes with summary statements and the benediction

Organ Postlude: "Worthy Is the Lamb"

Optional Closing

Narrator: If you have never given your life to Jesus, I invite you to do so tonight. We are going to play the song "Worthy Is the Lamb" again. When you hear this song you are invited to come to the front of church and to let Jesus be your shepherd, Savior, and king. Jesus is the only way to life, truth, and happiness. Maybe you have lived apart from the church for a while and God is calling you to come back to him. Maybe you have never been a part of a church before because you weren't raised that way or have been turned off by others. Jesus is calling you tonight. The Lamb says, "Come all you who hear. Come all you who are thirsty and have eternal life." There are many other shepherds in the world who would lead you astray. Jesus is the Good Shepherd. His paths are straight and true. Please don't leave until you have set your path straight with God. Our pastor and/or elders are available to help you. Please come.

Reset the stage with the cross and the lamb while the narrator is speaking.

Songs: "Shepherd of Love" and "Gentle Shepherd"

Narrator: Thank you to all who came forward today. Please stay here for the closing song and benediction. Afterward we will have some things to share together as well as literature for you. Our closing song is "Savior, Like a Shepherd Lead Us." Please stand and sing all the verses.

Closing Song: "Savior, Like a Shepherd Lead Us"

Pastor: Closes with summary statements and the benediction

Organ Postlude

7

Happy Birthday, Jesus

Notes to the Director

The program is divided into sections to allow the director to practice with smaller groups of students and leaders. Various props will be needed (see props page); begin early in the year. When entering the "Promises of God" or the "Promises Regarding the Second Coming of Christ" sections, a second narrator may be added so lines can be varied if necessary to allow for fewer children speaking roles.

List of Characters

Opening

Narrator—An adult or child who can speak clearly and slowly
Child 1—Three-year-old
Child 2—Three-year-old
Child 3—Four-year-old
Child 4—Four-year-old
Child 5—Five-year-old
Child 6—Five-year-old

Old Testament Skit

Father (Amos)—An adult
Son (Matthew)—Child in Sunday school
Rabbi—Adult or pastor of the church

New Testament skit

Mary
Angel 1
Joseph
Zechariah
Elizabeth
Angel 2
Choral Readers 1
Choral Readers 2
Isaiah

Modern Day Birthday Celebration

Child 1—Child from the Sunday school
Child 2—Child from the Sunday school
Mom—An adult
Dad—An adult
Grandpa—An adult
Grandma—An adult

Promises of God

Fifteen speakers from children in Sunday school

Promises Regarding the Second Coming of Christ

Seventeen speakers from children in Sunday school

Props
Opening
—Birthday cake with *candles* (battery-operated or cardboard with sequin "flames")
—8 1/2" x 11" picture of six children with their names on poster board
—Picture of Jesus

Old Testament Skit
—Costumes for the father, son, mother, and rabbi.
—Torah scroll with the words of the Ten Commandments printed on it. This can be made of two 1" dowels 12" long. The paper is 11" wide. The top of the paper is glued to one of the 12" pieces. The bottom of the paper is glued to the other 12" piece.
—A tabernacle is needed to house the scroll. It can be a box or cabinet.

New Testament Skit
Costumes will be needed for all the characters.

Modern Day Birthday Celebration
—Wrapped birthday presents for Child 1
—A birthday cake with *candles* (battery-operated or cardboard with sequin "flames")

Songs
Happy Birthday
Everybody Ought to Know
For God So Loved the World
Jesus Loves Me
Jesus Loves the Little Children
Silent Night! Holy Night!
What Child Is This?

The First Noel
Hark! the Herald Angels Sing
Joy to the World
Angels from the Realms of Glory
Standing on the Promises
Jesus Is Coming Again
Because He Lives
Family of God

Opening

The children begin processing from the rear of church where they have lined up by classes. The teachers lead the classes in, starting with the oldest classes and ending with the youngest. The Sunday school superintendent leads the processional holding a birthday cake with many candles. Use battery-operated candles or candles made from cardboard with "flames" of sequins or glitter. When the children come in everyone should be singing "Happy Birthday" to Jesus.

Song by Sunday school: "Happy Birthday to Jesus"

*Place the cake in a visible place
in the front of the sanctuary.*

Songs by the Sunday school children: "Everybody Ought to Know" and "For God So Loved the World"

Introduction to the Program:
Three- through Five-year-olds

Narrator: We would like to welcome you to the Sunday school Christmas program. The children reminded us that today is Jesus' birthday. The children are here to celebrate with us today the good news of their Savior and king Jesus.

They will be sharing with us how Jesus came into the world and why he is still remembered. The three- through five-year-olds will sing praises to their God and friend Jesus.

Have the name and a large (8 1/2" x 11") picture of each child on poster board tied to yarn around his or her neck.

Child 1: My name is _____. I am three (the child also holds up three fingers).

Child 2: My name is _____. I am three (the child also holds up three fingers).

Child 3: My name is _____. I am four (the child also holds up four fingers).

Child 4: My name is _____. I am four (the child also holds up four fingers).

Child 5: My name is _____. I am five (the child also holds up five fingers).

Child 6: My name is _____. I am five (the child also holds up five fingers).

All the three-through five-year-olds say together: This is Jesus. His birthday is today. We love him a lot. He loves us a lot, too.

Children sing: "Jesus Loves Me" and "Jesus Loves the Little Children"

Narrator: Long ago the Jews also celebrated birthdays. The Jews called it Bar Mitzvah when a boy reached age thirteen. It was a special way to celebrate a boy leaving boyhood and entering manhood. Let's watch as a Jewish family is preparing for the celebration of their oldest son's thirteenth birthday.

Old Testament Skit

Father: Come, my son, it's time to go to the temple for your Bar Mitzvah.

Matthew: Okay, Dad, I'm coming.

Father, mother, and son walk over to the temple scene and meet the priest.

Father: Hello, rabbi, how are you doing today?

Rabbi: Hello, Amos and Matthew. Are you ready for your Bar Mitzvah today?

Matthew: Yes, rabbi, I'm ready.

Rabbi: Well, relax, you'll do just fine.

Father: Come, mother, let's find a seat.

Father, mother, and son go and sit in the front row of the congregation.

Matthew: There are a lot of people here today, Dad. I'm a little nervous.

Father: That's okay, son, I was too for my Bar Mitzvah. You'll do just fine.

Rabbi: (Takes the scroll out of the tabernacle and places it open on the reading stand and then says:) Blessed art Thou, O Lord, our God, King of the Universe, Who has chosen us from all people and given us Thy Law. Today's reading is from Exodus 20. Matthew will be one of our readers. Today is his Bar Mitzvah.

Matthew comes forward and reads as follows:

Matthew: And God spoke all these words: "I am the LORD your God, who brought you out of Egypt, out of the land of slavery. You shall have no other gods before me. You shall not make for yourself an idol in the form of anything in heaven above or on the earth beneath or in the waters below. You shall not bow down to them or worship them; for I, the Lord your God, am a jealous God, punishing the children for the sin of the fathers to the third and fourth generation of those who hate me, but showing love to thousands who love me and keep my commandments. You shall not misuse the name of the Lord your God, for the Lord will not hold anyone guiltless who misuses his name. Remember the Sabbath day by keeping it holy. Six days you shall labor and do all your work, but the seventh day is a Sabbath to the Lord your God. On it you shall not do any work, neither you, nor your son or daughter, nor your manservant or maidservant, nor your animals, nor the alien within your gates. For in six days the Lord made the heavens and the earth, the sea, and all that is in them, but he rested on the seventh day. Therefore the Lord blessed the Sabbath day and made it holy. Honor your father and your mother, so that you may live long in the land the Lord your God is giving you. You shall not murder. You shall not commit adultery. You shall not steal. You shall not give false testimony against your neighbor. You shall not covet your neighbor's house. You shall not covet your neighbor's wife, or his manservant or maidservant, his ox or donkey, or anything that belongs to your neighbor" (Exod. 20:1–17).

Matthew returns to his seat after the reading.

Rabbi: My son, today is your thirteenth birthday. Up until now you may not have known the difference between right and wrong. But as of today you now accept responsibility for your actions. Amos, would you offer a prayer on your son's behalf?

Amos nods, stands, and says the following:

Amos: Almighty Father, Blessed be Thou, O Lord, our God, King of the Universe, Who has relieved me from responsibility for my child. Today my wife and I lift up our son to you. Grant him your wisdom in searching out truth, your knowledge in telling right from wrong, compassion to serve his neighbor, and love toward his brothers and sisters around him. Amen.

Rabbi: Matthew, you have prepared a short speech for us. Please read it now.

Matthew stands and says:

Matthew: Today is a milestone in my life. I pray that I may live up to the teachings found in the Torah and taught in this temple. I am ready to assume responsibility for my life and will do so with great humility and honor. May I be quick to learn, slow to speak, and also kind in heart.

Matthew sits down.

Rabbi: Blessed be Matthew, son of Amos. I pray that you will follow the commandments of the Lord our God and serve Him alone. At this time you have passed a milestone. Let us bring the service to a close and celebrate.

The rabbi returns the Torah scrolls to the tabernacle and all return to their seats.

New Testament Skit

Narrator: Christmas is Jesus' birthday. Many years ago God sent his Son Jesus to be born in this world. Jesus' birth was very special. He was born poor and died poor by the world's standards. But Jesus left behind a spiritual truth from God bigger than any man could dream. Jesus provided a way to break the sin barrier between God and us. He made it possible for us to have a personal relationship with a personal God. We want to reflect a few minutes with you, remembering the special events surrounding the birth of Jesus in the world. Please listen to the children as they tell us these events.

Song: "Silent Night! Holy Night!" sung by the three-year-olds through the fifth graders.

Narrator: Around 2000 years ago in a little city far away in the land of Israel, there lived a young woman named Mary.

Mary enters and goes to platform.

Narrator:	She was soon to be married to a carpenter named Joseph, a descendant of King David. One day Mary was sitting alone in her home.
	Mary sits down.
Narrator:	Suddenly an angel came and spoke with her.
Angel 1:	"Greetings, you who are highly favored! The Lord is with you" (Luke 1:28).
Mary:	Screams and then says, "You frighten me, go away, this is my house!"
Angel 1:	"Do not be afraid, Mary, you have found favor with God. You will be with child and give birth to a son, and you are to give him the name Jesus. He will be great and will be called the Son of the Most High. The Lord God will give him the throne of his father David, and he will reign over the house of Jacob forever; His kingdom will never end" (Luke 1:30–33).
Mary:	"How will this be . . . since I am a virgin?"
Angel 1:	"The Holy Spirit will come upon you, and the power of the Most High will overshadow you. So the holy one to be born will be called the Son of God. Even Elizabeth your relative is going to have a child in her old age, and she who was said to be barren is in her sixth month. For nothing is impossible with God" (Luke 1:34–37).
Mary:	"I am the Lord's servant. May it be to me as you have said" (Luke 1:38).

Mary stands and leaves the platform.

Narrator: Then Mary packed and went to see her relative Elizabeth. Both of them were going to have babies.

Elizabeth enters and sits down.
Mary runs in with bags packed with clothes.

Mary: Elizabeth, Elizabeth, guess what!
Elizabeth: Hi, Mary. It's good to see you!
Mary: An angel came and told me you were going to have a baby. I wanted to come and say "congratulations" to you and your husband Zechariah. Is he here?

Zechariah enters.

Mary: Congratulations, Zechariah!
Zechariah: Why, thank you, Mary.
Mary: Do you know what else the angel said?
Zech. and Eliza.: No, please tell us!
Mary: I'm going to have a baby, too!
Zech. and Eliza.: That's wonderful! Congratulations! We're so happy for you.
Narrator: The Bible then says that when Elizabeth's baby, who was John the Baptist, heard about Mary's baby, it leaped for joy inside her. Then Elizabeth said to Mary:
Elizabeth: "Blessed are you among women, and blessed is the child you will bear! But why am I so favored, that the mother of my Lord should come to me? As soon as the sound of your greeting reached

	my ears, the baby in my womb leaped for joy. Blessed is she who has believed that what the Lord has said to her will be accomplished!" (Luke 1:42b–45).
Narrator:	To celebrate the birth of Jesus in this world please stand and sing "What Child Is This?"
Congregational Hymn:	"What Child Is This?"

While the congregation is singing, the children prepare to sing.

Children sing: "The First Noel" and "Hark! the Herald Angels Sing"

Choral readers stand in groups of four or five and speak together.

Choral Readers 1: This is how the birth of Jesus Christ came about. His mother Mary was pledged to be married to Joseph, but before they came together, she was found to be with child through the Holy Spirit (Matt. 1:18).

Choral Readers 2: Because Joseph her husband was a righteous man and did not want to expose her to public disgrace, he had in mind to divorce her quietly. But after he had considered this, an angel of the Lord appeared to him in a dream and said, (Matt. 1:19–20a)

Joseph comes in and sits down. The angel of God comes in and stands by Joseph with arms raised.

Angel 2: "Joseph son of David, do not be afraid to take Mary home as your wife, because what is conceived in her is from the Holy Spirit. She will give birth to a son, and you are to give him the name Jesus, because he will save his people from their sins" (Matt. 1:20b–21).

The angel leaves and Joseph lies down.

Choral Readers 1: All this took place to fulfill what the Lord had said through the prophet Isaiah (Matt. 1:22).
Isaiah: The virgin will be with child and will give birth to a son, and they will call him Immanuel, which means, "God with us" (Matt. 1:23).

Joseph gets up. Mary comes on stage.
The two join hands and walk out to the back of church.

Choral Readers 2: When Joseph woke up, he did what the angel of the Lord commanded him and took Mary home as his wife (Matt. 1:24).
Choral Readers 1: But he had no union with her until she gave birth to a son. And he gave him the name Jesus (Matt. 1:25).
Songs by Sunday school children: "Joy to the World" and "Angels from the Realms of Glory"

Modern Day Birthday Celebration

Setting: Home atmosphere. Child 1 has many presents to open for his/her birthday. Mom is finishing the decorations for the cake and putting the candles on it.

Child 1:	Mom, can I open a present before Grandpa and Grandma get here?
Mom:	I know it's your birthday and you're excited, but you need to wait. Everyone will be here soon.
Child 2:	Mom, I want a present too.
Mom:	It's not your birthday, (Child's name); when you have a birthday, you can open presents, too.
Child 1:	But Mom, it's *my* birthday and I have so many presents. Can't I open just one before Grandpa and Grandma come?
Mom:	You need to wait, (Child 1). A long time ago the prophets in the Old Testament also had to wait what seemed forever for the baby Jesus to come and be born. The waiting makes special events even more special. Just as Jesus' birth involved waiting for God's right time, so you need to wait for the right time when all the people arrive.
Dad:	(Child 1), Mom is right. You are very special to us, and we love you enough to say, "Wait for the right time."
Child 1:	Okay, but I wish they would hurry up.
Child 2:	(Child 1's name), what do you think this one is?

The children keep talking about the present to each other when someone knocks at the door.

Child 1:	I'll get it.

Child 1 runs over and opens the door for Grandpa and Grandma. Grandpa and Grandma should have presents in hand for Child 1.

Child 1:	Hi, Grandpa and Grandma! Mom, Dad, they're here! Now can I open my presents? Hurry, Grandpa and Grandma!
Grandpa:	Hi, (name of mom and dad). (Child 1's name) is sure excited about his/her birthday.
Dad:	(He/She) certainly is. (Child 1) could hardly wait until you got here. Come, have a seat over here.

Everyone sits down around Child 1. Make sure Child 1 is visible to the congregation.

Mom:	Before you begin with the presents, tell us again, why are presents important to our family?
Child 2:	Because we get toys to play with.
Dad:	Yes, but there is another reason.
Child 1:	Because God loved us so much he sent Jesus to the world to save us from sin.
Dad:	That's right. Besides, we love you, too, so we celebrate the day God brought you into the world to be with us. (Child 2), can you tell us what John 3:16 says?
Child 2:	"For God so loved the world that he gave his one and only Son, that whoever believes in him shall not perish but have eternal life" (John 3:16).
Mom:	Very good, (name of Child 2). (Name of Child 1), we were very thankful to Jesus when he brought you to us. We want good things for you just as God gives us good things. God has given us eternal life. God gives us his word

which is always true. In his word are many promises for those of us who trust in him. Listen to some of the children share a few of these promises of God with us.

Promises of God

*Each child holds a card
with a saying about his or her verse.*

Card Saying	Speaker	Verse
God Says Yes!	1	2 Corinthians 1:20a—For no matter how many promises God has made, they are "Yes" in Christ.
Trustworthy	2	Joshua 23:14b—You know that with all your heart and soul that not one of all the good promises the LORD your God gave you has failed. Every promise has been fulfilled; not one has failed.
Great Promises	3	2 Peter 1:4—Through these he has given us his very great and precious promises, so that through them you may participate in the divine nature and escape the corruption in the world caused by evil desires.
God's Covenant	4	Jeremiah 31:33—"This is the covenant I will make with the house of Israel after that time," declares the LORD. "I will put my

Given All We Need	5	law in their minds and write it on their hearts. I will be their God, and they will be my people."
		2 Peter 1:3—His divine power has given us everything we need for life and godliness through our knowledge of him who called us by his own glory and goodness.
Answers Prayers	6	Mark 11:24—"Therefore I tell you, whatever you ask for in prayer, believe that you have received it, and it will be yours."
Grants Hearts' Desires	7	Psalm 37:4—Delight yourself in the LORD and he will give you the desires of your heart.
Jesus Fills Our Needs	8	Matthew 7:7—"Ask and it will be given to you; seek and you will find; knock and the door will be opened to you."
Ask In Jesus' Name	9	John 14:14—"You may ask me for anything in my name, and I will do it."
Ask The Father	10	Matthew 18:19—"Again, I tell you that if two of you on earth agree about anything you ask for, it will be done for you by my Father in heaven."
Be Humble/Seek God	11	2 Chronicles 7:14—"If my people, who are called by my name, will humble themselves and pray and seek my face and turn from their wicked ways,

		then will I hear from heaven and will forgive their sin and will heal their land."
All Things Work For Good	12	Romans 8:28—And we know that in all things God works for the good of those who love him, who have been called according to his purpose.
Help In Trouble	13	Psalm 50:15—"And call upon me in the day of trouble; I will deliver you, and you will honor me."
God Watches Over Us	14	Psalm 121:4–5—Indeed, he who watches over Israel will neither slumber nor sleep. The LORD watches over you— the LORD is your shade at your right hand.
God Grants Us Strength	15	Isaiah 40:31—But those who hope in the LORD will renew their strength. They will soar on wings like eagles; they will run and not grow weary, they will walk and not be faint.

Modern Day
Birthday Celebration Continued

Song by the Sunday school:	"Standing on the Promises"
Dad:	Sometimes we make promises to you. We try to keep them all but parents aren't always perfect. God is perfect. When God makes a promise, he will

keep it. Now when you open the presents, remember we give you these things because of the joy you bring us and the happiness you give to God.

The family sings "Happy Birthday" to Child 1.

Dad: Let's open presents!
Child 1: Okay!!!
Narrator: At this time the offering will be received. This year's offering will be given to the Sunday school's missionary program of our church.

Offering—Taken by the deacons

Offertory Prayer

Song by the
Sunday school: "Jesus Is Coming Again"

Narrator: Jesus didn't remain a baby in Bethlehem. He is alive today and reigns supreme at God's right hand. The children have just sung about Jesus' Second Coming to the world. Please open your hymn books to number___, "Because He Lives," standing to sing all the verses.

Song by the congregation—"Because He Lives"

Promises Regarding the Second Coming of Christ

Narrator: Jesus will return again someday. When he does, Christians will be joined together to celebrate his greatness with a huge birthday party that will never end. Until he does, we preach the good news of Jesus to the world around us. When Jesus returns, God tells us this:

Card Saying	Speaker	Verse
God Will Keep Us Safe	1	2 Timothy 1:12b—I know whom I have believed, and am convinced that he is able to guard what I have entrusted to him for that day.
Salvation	2	Acts 2:38–39—Peter replied, "Repent and be baptized, every one of you, in the name of Jesus Christ so that your sins may be forgiven. And you will receive the gift of the Holy Spirit. The promise is for you and your children and for all who are far off—for all whom the Lord our God will call."
Crown of Life	3	James 1:12—Blessed is the man who perseveres under trial, because when he has stood the test, he will receive the crown of life that God has promised to those who love him.
Crown of Life	4	Revelation 2:10—Do not be afraid of what you are about to suffer. I tell you, the devil will put some of you in prison

to test you, and you will suffer persecution for ten days. Be faithful, even to the point of death, and I will give you the crown of life.

Jesus Is Coming	5	John 14:28—"You heard me say, 'I am going away and I am coming back to you.' If you loved me, you would be glad that I am going to the Father, for the Father is greater than I."
We Don't Know When	6	Matthew 24:42—Therefore keep watch, because you do not know on what day your Lord will come.
God's Timing	7	2 Peter 3:8—But do not forget this one thing, dear friends: With the Lord a day is like a thousand years, and a thousand years are like a day.

Card Saying	**Speaker**	**Verse**
Not Slow	8	2 Peter 3:9—The Lord is not slow in keeping his promise, as some understand slowness. He is patient with you, not wanting anyone to perish, but everyone to come to repentance.
Day of the Lord Is Like a Thief	9	2 Peter 3:10—But the day of the Lord will come like a thief. The heavens will disappear

Jesus Will Return	10	with a roar; the elements will be destroyed by fire, and the earth and everything in it will be laid bare.

Acts 1:11—"Men of Galilee," they said, "why do you stand here looking into the sky? This same Jesus, who has been taken from you into heaven, will come back in the same way you have seen him go into heaven." |
Jesus Will Return with Power	11	Mark 14:62—"I am," said Jesus. "And you will see the Son of Man sitting at the right hand of the Mighty One and coming on the clouds of heaven."
Be Ready!	12	Luke 12:40—"You also must be ready, because the Son of Man will come at an hour when you do not expect him."
Come as Lightning	13	Matthew 24:27—For as the lightning comes from the east and flashes to the west, so will be the coming of the Son of Man.
Returning on the Clouds	14	Revelation 1:7—Look, he is coming with the clouds, and every eye will see him, even those who pierced him; and all the peoples of the earth will mourn because of him. So shall it be! Amen.

New Earth	**15**	2 Peter 3:13—But in keeping with his promise we are looking forward to a new heaven and a new earth, the home of righteousness.
Redeemer Lives	**16**	Job 19:25—I know that my Redeemer lives, and that in the end he will stand upon the earth.
I Am the Resurrection	**17**	John 11:25—Jesus said to her, "I am the resurrection and the life. He who believes in me will live, even though he dies."

Closing

Narrator: The promises the children spoke of are for you today. Are you ready to receive the promises God has offered? Are you ready to celebrate Jesus' birthday? Have you taken Christ to be your personal Savior and Lord? To date, all things promised by God have come true. Now, only the promises made which affect the return of Christ remain unanswered. But we don't have long to decide whether or not to be a part of God's family. Know where you stand with God. If your future is uncertain and you don't know Jesus personally as Savior and Lord, then I invite you to meet Jesus today. Don't leave until you speak with me or the pastor. Now please stand as we sing together "Family of God."

Congregational
Song: "Family of God"

Closing comments, prayer and benediction by the pastor

All Sunday school children say together:
"Happy Birthday, Jesus!"

Organ Postlude

8

Of Men and Angels

Notes to the Director

Program Welcome

Begin the program with the youngest children since they have such short attention spans.

Program Introduction

Angel 1—Michael and Angel 2—Gabriel do the majority of the narration. In the introduction Michael is looking for Gabriel; Gabriel enters by crash landing off stage. Sound effects records from libraries are a good resource for finding the noise you need. Some synthesizers can also produce sounds. A third option would be to "crash" pots, pans and cooking utensils together.

Daniel in the Lions' Den

Plan carefully so you can change scenery quickly with the fewest props. Children could play the role of lions. A creative seamstress could design costumes for the children.

The Temple Scene

Two sections need to be made: one for the temple with an altar and incense table and one for the outer courts where the people wait. Boys and girls play the nonspeaking roles.

The Announcement of Jesus' Birth

A house room setting will be needed for two scenes: when the angel appears to Elizabeth in the temple and when the angel appears to Mary in the announcement of Jesus' birth.

Jesus' Birth Scene

Reset the stage with the manger and shepherd scenery. After the angel appears to Mary, she should exit and join Joseph in the rear of church; they then walk down the aisle for enrollment in Bethlehem.

Peter's Escape from Jail

You can use the same house scene as in the previous two sections. Also use the jail scenery here. There are four guards: two alongside Peter in jail and two standing watch just outside the jail. The angel and Peter pause to talk with each other between the guards in the jail and those outside. After the angel and Peter pass by the second pair of guards, the angel disappears and Peter goes to the house where others are praying for him.

Props

Daniel in the Lions' Den

Three scenes are necessary:
1. A house scene where Daniel is writing at a table
2. A palace scene where communication with the king takes place
3. The lions' den scene

The Temple

A temple setting—could be the same as the palace setting but with divider added to separate the outer court (in which the people wait) from the temple interior (where Zechariah prepares the incense)

The Announcement of Jesus' Birth

Three scenes are necessary:
1. A home scene for Mary—could be the same home scene used for Daniel
2. An outdoor scene with sheep
3. A manger scene for Jesus' birth with a straw or hay manger—include the innkeeper's house which could be the home scene used earlier

Peter's Escape from Jail

1. A jail scene with straw or hay floor
2. Handcuffs which can come off easily
3. The house scene—could be the one used earlier

Costumes for all parts are necessary. Include swords and/or spears for the guards.

Songs

The B-I-B-L-E
Stop and Go
I Have the Joy
Happy All the Time
Happiness Is
Away in a Manger
Silent Night! Holy Night!
Angels, From the Realms of Glory
Angels We Have Heard On High
Jesus Is All the World to Me
Angels (by Amy Grant)
A Thousand Angels

List of Characters
Program Introduction

Angel 1
Angel 2

Daniel in the Lions' Den

Narrator
Naboth
Haman
King Darius
Guards: Nonspeaking roles
Daniel

The Temple Scene

Zechariah
Several children for the outer court setting (4–20 children)

The Announcement of Jesus' Birth

Mary

Jesus' Birth Scene

Speakers 1–14
Angel Choir: 4–10 children to speak in unison
Shepherds: One speaking role and 3 or 4 nonspeaking roles

Peter's Escape from Jail

Speakers 1–10
4 Guards: Nonspeaking roles
Peter
Mary
Rhoda
House Member 1
House Members: Nonspeaking roles - 4 or 5 children

Closing

Speakers 1–9

The roles of angels 1 & 2 and the narrator should be the same persons throughout the play

—Of Men and Angels—
Program Welcome

Three-year-olds say in unison:
    Through all the words we say,
    We hope you enjoy your stay.
    We came here to bring
    Praise to our king!

Four-year-olds say in unison:
    We welcome you, moms and dads,
    We welcome you, grandmas and grandpas,
    We welcome you, brothers and sisters,
    We welcome you, friends and relatives,
    You came here to hear us talk and sing,
    We came to praise Jesus to whom we cling.

Songs by the preschoolers: "The B-I-B-L-E" and "Stop and Go!"

Program Introduction

Two angels narrate the program from a high point in the front of the sanctuary.

Angel 1:   Gab . . . Gab . . . Gabriel? Where are you? Gabriel? . . . Is that you coming?

Angel 1, looks off stage, straining to see Gabriel. Sounds of angel 2 coming are heard. Play sound effects record of a plane crash landing. Other options would be using a synthesizer or pots and pans crashing together. Then have a few minutes of silence.

Angel 2:   Michael, I'll be right there. Give me a minute to pull myself together.

Gabriel slowly walks over to Michael.

Angel 1:	By the way, Gabriel, how are you doing with your flight lessons?
Angel 2:	Pretty good, actually. Flying isn't the problem. Landing is a killer! I need to study harder.
Angel 1:	Gabriel, as you know, we have been actively involved in the lives of humans for some time. God has used us to protect Christians, help people in trouble, and bring messages of happiness.
Angel 2:	You're right, Michael! Remember the time a while back when Daniel had to face those lions? It sure was good to see God's purpose overcome man's evil intentions.
Angel 1:	Let's listen to the story.

Daniel in the Lions' Den

Narrator:	Many years ago in a land far away, when Darius was king over the Medes and Persians, there lived a man called Daniel.

Daniel enters and sits at a table, pretending to be writing.

Narrator:	Daniel was an upright man. He obeyed God and lived by God's standards. Because Daniel was a great leader King Darius appointed him to be one of three administrators.

Two administrators enter and stand near Daniel, talking to each other.

Haman: Naboth, we need to do something about how much power the king has given Daniel.

Naboth: I know. And another thing: the king likes Daniel more than us.

Haman: We are administrators just as Daniel. We have the same title, but the king likes Daniel more. That needs to change. Come here, I have a plan.

The two huddle close together and pretend to talk over a plan. Then they separate and Naboth speaks to Haman.

Naboth: That's a good plan, Haman. Let's do it!

Naboth and Haman walk over to the king.

Haman: King Darius, live forever.

King Darius: Yes, Haman, what do you want?

Haman: We need a new law to show everyone how great you are.

Naboth: Even as we speak, people in your kingdom are praying to many gods. They give their gods too high a position. You need to show them you are king above all gods.

King Darius: What are you proposing?

Haman: We think you should decree that anyone who prays to any god or man during the next 30 days, except to you, O King, shall be thrown in the lions' den.

Naboth: Now, O king, issue the decree in writing as a law of the Medes and Persians so it cannot be altered.

King Darius: Very well, draw up the law on paper. I'll sign it.

They hand the king a document. The king signs it. Naboth and Haman leave the king's presence.

Haman: We have Daniel now! Three times a day Daniel prays to his God upstairs near the window facing Jerusalem. Let's get the guards.

The men leave, Daniel goes to the window, kneels and prays to God. While Daniel is praying, Haman, Naboth and the guards enter Daniel's house.

Naboth: Arrest that man! Bring him to the king.

The guards take Daniel to the king.

Haman: O king, live forever.
King Darius: Enter.
Haman: Remember the law you signed? Well, Daniel has broken it. He was caught praying to his God. He ignores your laws. Send him to the lions.
Naboth: Yes, off to the lions with Daniel.
King Darius: Wait. This is my best administrator. We can't kill him. Besides, he's my friend.
Haman: O king, you must send Daniel to the lions. Not even you, the king over all Babylon, can change a law of the Medes and Persians once it is made.
King Darius: Very well, but wait until evening.

Haman and Naboth leave, King Darius walks over to Daniel and says,

King Darius: Daniel, I'm so sorry. You were a good friend to me, but I see no way out of this.

Daniel: I am still a good friend. God will provide a way for me.

Turn off lights.

Set up the stage for the lions' den scene. Four or five children play the roles of hungry lions. One child plays the role of an angel who waits until the appropriate time to enter and close the lions' mouths.

Turn on lights.

Naboth: Here we are. Guards, take Daniel and throw him to the lions.

The guards throw Daniel to the children who are pretending to be lions.

Haman: Let's go, Naboth. Daniel is history. Now we can carry out our plans. First let's have a party.

King Darius: Daniel, "May your God, whom you serve continually, rescue you" (Dan. 6:16b).

Angel 1 appears in the lions' den and comforts Daniel while commanding the lions not to eat Daniel.

Angel 1: Lions, in the name of the Most High God, you are not to touch a hair on this man's head. Daniel, don't be afraid. I have been sent of God to close the lions' mouths. You are innocent before God and man.

Daniel: Thank-you, Lord God.

Turn off lights.

Narrator:	Then the king returned to his palace and spent the night without eating and without any entertainment being brought to him. And he could not sleep. At the first light of dawn, the king got up and hurried to the lions' den (Dan. 6:18–19).

Lights come on and the king rushes to the den.

King Darius:	Daniel, Daniel, are you okay? "Daniel, servant of the living God, has your God, whom you serve continually, been able to rescue you from the lions?" (Dan. 6:20).
Daniel:	"O king, live forever! My God sent his angel, and he shut the mouths of the lions. They have not hurt me, because I was found innocent in his sight. Nor have I ever done any wrong before you, O king" (Dan. 6:21–22).
King Darius:	Guards, get Daniel out of there. Find the men responsible for this.

The two guards leave and return with Haman and Naboth, while two other guards help Daniel out of the lions' den.

Clear stage.

Narrator:	Then King Darius wrote to all the peoples, nations and men of every language throughout the land: "May you prosper greatly! I issue a decree that in every part of my kingdom people must fear and reverence the God of Daniel. For he is the living God and he endures

forever; his kingdom will not be destroyed, his dominion will never end. He rescues and he saves; He performs signs and wonders in the heavens and on the earth. He has rescued Daniel from the power of the lions" (Daniel 6:25–27).

Turn off lights. Clear the stage. Then turn lights on.

Angel 1: That was exciting! I really enjoy the good old days.

Angel 2: Me, too. I think when Daniel came out from the lions' den he may have wanted to sing a song like this:

Song by
Sunday school: "I Have the Joy," "Happy All the Time," or "Happiness Is"

The Temple Scene

Angel 1: One of our most exciting times was when God told us to announce the birth of his son Jesus. Wasn't that fun?

Angel 2: It sure was! Do you think we could relive that period of history? I sure would like to see the story of Jesus' birth again.

Angel 1: Sure, let's do it. Why not?

Set the stage for the temple scene. Have Zechariah preparing incense for the altar in the temple. Boys and girls should play the role of the people standing outside the temple waiting for Zechariah.

Narrator: In the time of Herod king of Judea there was a priest named Zechariah, who belonged to the priestly division of Abijah; his wife Elizabeth was also a descendant of Aaron. Both of them were upright in the sight of God, observing all the Lord's commandments and regulations blamelessly. But they had no children, because Elizabeth was barren; and they were both well along in years. Once when Zechariah's division was on duty and he was serving as priest before God, he was chosen by lot, according to the custom of the priesthood, to go into the temple of the Lord and burn incense. And when the time for the burning of incense came, all the assembled worshipers were praying outside (Luke 1:5–10).

Angel 2 enters and stands near Zechariah. When Zechariah sees Angel 2, he acts startled and afraid.

Angel 2: "Do not be afraid, Zechariah; your prayer has been heard. Your wife Elizabeth will bear you a son, and you are to give him the name John. He will be a joy and delight to you, and many will rejoice because of his birth, for he will be great in the sight of the Lord. He is never to take wine or other fermented drink, and he will be filled with the Holy Spirit even from birth. Many of the people of Israel will he bring back to the Lord their God. And he will go on before the Lord, in the spirit and power of Elijah, to turn the hearts of the fathers to their children and the disobedient to the wisdom of the righteous—to make ready a people prepared for the Lord" (Luke 1:13–17).

Zechariah: I don't know who you are, but I think you have the wrong man.

Angel 2: I don't have the wrong man. I was sent here from God.

Zechariah: Now listen here, mister. I am an old man and my wife is too old to have children. Now check your direction map and I'm sure you will find God meant for you to be somewhere else, speaking to someone else.

Angel 2: "I am Gabriel. I stand in the presence of God, and I have been sent to speak to you and to tell you this good news. And now you will be silent and not able to speak until the day this happens, because you did not believe my words, which will come true at their proper time" (Luke 1:19–20).

Angel 2 leaves.

Narrator: Meanwhile, the people were waiting for Zechariah and wondering why he stayed so long in the temple. When he came out, he could not speak to them. They realized he had seen a vision in the temple, for he kept making signs to them but remained unable to speak.

Zechariah points up to the sky and back to the temple several times while saying nothing.

Several children say at different times:
"Zechariah, what happened to you?"

Other children say at different times:
"He has seen a vision."

Turn off lights and clear the stage. Set up for the Angel and Mary scene.

The Announcement of Jesus' Birth

Mary is sitting alone in a room, folding clothes.

Narrator: In the sixth month, God sent the angel Gabriel to Nazareth, a town in Galilee, to a virgin pledged to be married to a man named Joseph, a descendant of David. The virgin's name was Mary (Luke 1:26–27).

Angel 2 enters and surprises Mary.

Angel 2: "Greetings, you who are highly favored! The Lord is with you" (Luke 1:28).

Mary acts afraid and looks for an exit.

Angel 2: "Do not be afraid, Mary, you have found favor with God. You will be with child and give birth to a son, and you are to give him the name Jesus. He will be great and will be called the Son of the Most High. The Lord God will give him the throne of his father David, and he will reign over the house of Jacob forever; his kingdom will never end" (Luke 1:30–33).

Mary: How did you get in here? How did you know my name? How can I have a baby? I don't have a husband and have never been with a man.

Angel 2: "The Holy Spirit will come upon you, and the power of the Most High will over-

	shadow you. So the hold one to be born will be called the Son of God. Even Elizabeth your relative is going to have a child in her old age, and she who was said to be barren is in her sixth month. For nothing is impossible with God" (Luke 1:35–37).
Mary:	I am the Lord's servant. May it be to me as you have said.

Turn off lights and clear the stage for Jesus' birth.

Jesus' Birth Scene

Speaker 1:	In those days Caesar Augustus issued a decree that a census should be taken of the entire Roman world.
Speaker 2:	This was the first census that took place while Quirinius was governor of Syria.
Speaker 3:	And everyone went to his own town to register.
Speaker 4:	So Joseph also went up from the town of Nazareth in Galilee to Judea, to Bethlehem the town of David, because he belonged to the house and line of David.
Speaker 5:	He went there to register with Mary, who was pledged to be married to him and was expecting a child.
Speaker 6:	While they were there, the time came for the baby to be born.
Speaker 7:	And she gave birth to her firstborn, a son. She wrapped him in cloths and placed him in a manger, because there was no room for them in the inn.

The children sit down. Mary and Joseph act out the skit while "No Room" is sung by a soloist.

Mary and Joseph should enter from the back and walk slowly to the front of the sanctuary. They pause by the inn and knock on the door. The innkeeper comes out, shakes his head "no", and points to the stable. Mary and Joseph go over to the stable where she kneels by the manger, Joseph stands at her side.

Turn out the lights. Have the shepherds enter and take positions with sheep. Mary and Joseph stay where they are.

Aim lights on the shepherds and the sheep.

Songs by the Sunday school: "Away in a Manger," "Silent Night," "Angels, From the Realms of Glory"

Speaker 8: And there were shepherds living out in the fields nearby, keeping watch over their flocks at night (Luke 2:8).

An angel appears, lights shine on the angel and shepherds act afraid.

Speaker 9: An angel of the Lord appeared to them, and the glory of the Lord shone around them, and they were terrified (Luke 2:9).

Angel 1: "Do not be afraid. I bring you good news of great joy that will be for all the people. Today in the town of David a Savior has been born to you; he is Christ the Lord. This will be a sign to you: You will find a baby wrapped in cloths and lying in a manger" (Luke 2:10–12).

Many angels (4–10 children, depending on your Sunday school size) join angel 1 and say verse 14 together three times.

All Angels: "Glory to God in the highest, and on earth peace to men on whom his favor rests" (Luke 2:14).

Angels leave shepherds.

Shepherd: Come on. Hurry! We need to go to Bethlehem to see the baby the angels were talking about.

Speakers 10–14 line up to speak. The shepherds act out the story as the speakers say their verses.

Speaker 10: So they hurried off and found Mary and Joseph, and the baby, who was lying in the manger (Luke 2:16).

Speaker 11: When they had seen him, they spread the word concerning what had been told them about this child (Luke 2:17).

Speaker 12: And all who heard it were amazed at what the shepherds said to them (Luke 2:18).

Speaker 13: But Mary treasured up all those things and pondered them in her heart (Luke 2:19).

Speaker 14: The shepherds returned, glorifying and praising God for all the things they had heard and seen, which were just as they had been told (Luke 2:20).

Songs by Sunday school: "While Shepherds Watched Their Flocks by Night," "Hark! the Herald Angels Sing"

Angel 1: The children would like you to stand and join them in singing "Angels We Have Heard on High," number _____ in your songbooks.

Congregational Song: "Angels We Have Heard on High"

Angel 2: You may be seated while the offering is received.

Offering

Offertory played by youth in Sunday school.

Offertory Prayer

Peter's Escape From Jail

Angel 1: The Christmas story was definitely the highlight of our ministry with God and his people.

Angel 2: It sure was. However, I'm happy God still involves us in the world of men and angels after Jesus died, rose from the dead, and returned to heaven.

Angel 1: Yes. God could have ended it all there but he still wants people to come to know him as their Savior and Lord.

Angel 2: I remember a time when King Herod tried to kill the apostle Peter. King Herod was mad because Peter was spreading news to others about Jesus being alive. Weren't you involved in breaking Peter out of jail, Michael?

Angel 1: I did what God told me to do. Watch my friends as they show you how it was done.

Set up the stage for the jail scene.
Speakers 1–7 line up to speak.

Speaker 1: It was about this time that King Herod arrested some who belonged to the church, intending to persecute them (Acts 12:1).

Speaker 2: He had James, the brother of John, put to death with the sword (Acts 12:2).

Speaker 3: When he saw that this pleased the Jews, he proceeded to seize Peter also. This happened during the Feast of Unleavened Bread (Acts 12:3).

Speaker 4: After arresting him, he put him in prison, handing him over to be guarded by four squads of four soldiers each. Herod intended to bring him out for public trial after the Passover (Acts 12:4).

Speaker 5: So Peter was kept in prison, but the church was earnestly praying to God for him (Acts 12:5).

Speaker 6: The night before Herod was to bring him to trial, Peter was sleeping between two soldiers, bound with two chains, and sentries stood guard at the entrances (Acts 12:6).

Speaker 7: Suddenly an angel of the Lord appeared and a light shone in the cell. He struck Peter on the side and woke him up (Acts. 12:7a).

Angel 1 slips in quietly and hits Peter on the side and wakes him up. The two guards alongside Peter stay sleeping.

Angel 1: "Quick, get up" (Acts 12:7b).

The chains fall off Peter's wrists.

Angel 1: "Put on your clothes and sandals" (Acts 12:8a).

Angel 1 hands Peter his robe and sandals. Peter puts them on and follows the angel.

Peter: What's happening here? Wait; am I dreaming?

Peter takes the angel's arm and stops the angel.

Angel 1: No, you're not dreaming. Now hurry, Peter; don't wake up the guards.

Peter: Who are you? I know, I'm having a vision. I'm really asleep in the prison and this is all pretend, right?

Angel 1: Wrong, Peter! This is real, we are leaving the prison. I am an angel sent from God to deliver you from the hand of King Herod. Now come quickly, we must pass by one more set of guards.

They walk by the second set of guards, then Angel 1 disappears.

Peter: "Now I know without a doubt that the Lord sent his angel and rescued me from Herod's clutches and from everything the Jewish people were anticipating" (Acts 12:11).

Speakers 8–10 enter. They should read loudly, clearly, and slowly. Allow acting time.

Children act out parts as the readers say the verses.

Speaker 8: When this had dawned on him, he went to the house of Mary . . . where

	many people had gathered and were praying (Acts 12:2).
Speaker 9:	Peter knocked at the outer entrance, and a servant girl named Rhoda came to answer the door (Acts 12:13).
Speaker 10:	When she recognized Peter's voice, she was so overjoyed she ran back without opening it (Acts 12:14a).
Rhoda:	Peter is at the door, Peter is at the door!
Mary:	You must be out of your mind. It can't be.
Rhoda:	No, it is Peter! I saw him. I really saw him.
Mary:	Rhoda, listen to me. Peter is still in jail. That is why we are praying for him here. You have just interrupted our prayers. That's rude. It must be something else.

Peter keeps on knocking at the door.

Mary:	What is that noise?
House member 1:	It sounds like someone knocking at the door.
Mary:	It couldn't be Peter, could it?
Rhoda:	I told you so. I told you so!

All leave to find Peter at the door.

All:	It is Peter. It is Peter!

*Peter quiets them and briefly comes in
to explain what has happened that night.*

Peter: It's me, Peter! An angel of the Lord rescued me from prison. "Tell James and the brothers about this" (Acts 12:17b). I need to go now. See you all later.

Turn off lights and reset the stage for the closing scene.

Angel 2: There is a beautiful song that Peter may have felt like singing to express his joy to God for breaking him out of jail. It's called "Jesus Is All the World to Me," page _____ in your hymn books. Please rise as we sing all the verses.

Congregational Song: "Jesus Is All the World to Me"

Angel 2: Thank-you. You may be seated.

Closing

Angel 1: Well, we covered a lot of ground. I wonder what God wants us to do today?

Angel 2: I'm sure we will be busy helping God's people in some way. Will you tell me the duties of angels again?

Angel 1: Amy Grant sang a song called "Angels." Listen to the words. It describes some of our duties.

Either play the song by Amy Grant "Angels," or have soloist sing it.

Solo: "Angels"

Angel 2: That was beautiful. Thank-you.
Angel 1: Listen to the boys and girls. They have

learned some Bible verses which will help us remember our daily duties.

Speakers 1–9 come forward to speak holding cards which summarize their verse(s).

No.	Card Saying	Verse(s)
1	Angels Worship God	Nehemiah 9:6—You alone are the LORD. You made the heavens, even the highest heavens, and all their starry host, the earth and all that is on it, the seas and all that is in them. You give life to everything, and the multitudes of heaven worship you. Hebrews 1:6 says – Let all God's angels worship him.
2	Ministering Spirits	Hebrews 1:14—Are not all angels ministering spirits sent to serve those who will inherit salvation?
3	Obey God	Psalm 103:20–21—Praise the LORD, you his angels, you mighty ones who do his bidding, who obey his word. Praise the LORD, all his heavenly hosts, you his servants who do his will.
4	Sort Good from Evil	Matthew 13:41–43—The Son of Man will send out his angels, and they will weed out his kingdom everything that causes sin and all who do evil.

		They will throw them into the fiery furnace, where there will be weeping and gnashing of teeth. Then the righteous will shine like the sun in the kingdom of their Father.
5	Protect God's Children	Psalm 34:7—The angel of the Lord encamps around those who fear him, and he delivers them.
6	Guard God's People	Psalm 91:11–12—For he will command his angels concerning you to guard you in all your ways; they will lift you up in their hands, so that you will not strike your foot against a stone.
7	Assigned to God's Children	Matthew 18:10—See that you do not look down on one of these little ones. For I tell you that their angels in heaven always see the face of my Father in heaven.
8	Not to be Worshiped	Revelation 22:8–9—I, John, am the one who heard and saw these things. And when I had heard and seen them, I fell down to worship at the feet of the angel who had been showing them to me. But he said to me, "Do not do it! I am a fellow servant with you and with your brothers the prophets and of all who keep

9 Number in the Thousands	the words of this book. Worship God!"
	Hebrews 12:22—But you have come to Mount Zion, to the heavenly Jerusalem, the city of the living God. You have come to thousands upon thousands of angels in joyful assembly.

Speakers 1–9 sit down.

Angel 2: After what the boys and girls said, I think we will be very busy!

Angel 1: That's right, but I wouldn't have it any other way!

Closing comments by the pastor

Narrator or pastor: Please stand and sing "A Thousand Angels," number ____ in your hymn book.

Benediction

Organ postlude